"I no longer call you servants, because a servant does not know his master's business. Instead, I have called you friends, for everything that I learned from my Father I have made known to you." John 15:15, NIV

— Contents —

Introduction 7

Chapter 1
The Gospel According to Bart 11

Chapter 2
When Good Isn't Good Enough 19

Chapter 3
Angry With God 27

Chapter 4
Seeing Clearly 34

Chapter 5
Life on a Limb 43

Chapter 6
Too Good to Pass Up 50

Chapter 7
To the Highest Bidder 57

Chapter 8
The Good, the Bad, and the Ugly 64

Chapter 9
Entangled with Grace 71

Chapter 10
Godzilla 79

Postscript 88

References 90

—— Introduction ——

I was with a friend at the Getty Museum in Los Angeles. We were there to see the art of Mexican photographer, Graciela Iturbide. We began our tour of her collection, entitled *La Danza de la Cabrita* (The Goat's Dance). It was considered to be quite an expensive exhibit. I'm not certain how one determines the worth of a collection of photos I could have easily taken in my backyard, but I'm sure part of the value is estimated by the popularity of the artist. That popularity is usually earned by having a "good eye" as a photographer. Whatever the reasons, I was there to be impressed.

Now before you start thinking I'm cultured and have a taste for the fine arts, I was bored from the beginning with the framed photograph named *Angel Woman*. Iturbide had photographed a woman walking along a cliff's edge wearing a traditional native Mexican dress while holding a boom box in her right hand. The black and white photo was taken from behind the woman.

The tour guide asked us to look at the picture and share our thoughts with the group. One person talked about how the lighting in the picture made him focus on the bright spots (yeah, he was a genius). Another person talked about the contrast between all of the natural wonder in the picture with the modern boom box in her hand (what an observation!). Then some lady talked about how mysterious the woman in the picture was because you couldn't see her face (Ding! Ding! Ding! What do we have for her, Johnny?). They were killing me! They might as well have commented on the dust resting on top of the picture frame. ... Way too much analysis for something so simple. They all seemed to be stating the overly obvious.

The guide then asked me to chime in and I couldn't resist. "This is by far the best photograph of the exhibit. The boom box looks like something from VH1's 'I Love the Eighties' show." Then something happened during my satirical commentary. As I continued to stare at the picture, I couldn't escape my evolving impression of the woman in the photo. It seemed so obvious, but the thought was too embarrassing to mention aloud. I was comfortable being the funny guy, and to give a serious analysis would go against the grain of what I considered to be entertaining, but I just couldn't hold it in any longer.

"She ... she looks like a he ... and he looks like a Samurai. Check out the outfit. Look at the masculine 'T' shape of her upper body, and the long Samurai hair. Yep, all she is missing is a sword." Yes, I was serious. I couldn't help it. It's what I saw. Needless to say, I was asked to leave the tour.

See what happens when you stare at a picture long enough? It's not that the photo was as abstract as an inkblot, but there was enough ambiguity to walk away with my own interpretation. Why couldn't anyone else see the Samurai? Did they not look long enough? Did they just say what they knew the tour guide wanted to hear? Were they conformists? Perhaps life is similar to my museum experience. We can all look at the exact same thing and interpret something completely different.

Get the Picture?

This episode at the museum reminds me of my experience of staring at what might be the single most debatable exhibit in the whole world: God. I must admit, my first picture of God was created by what others had told me about Him. I had never carefully looked for myself. I was encouraged not to ask too many questions—just believe in Him. 'Love and serve Him, or else you're going to get it in the end'. That was difficult to accept because I had so many questions. There was so much mystery surrounding God that I often found myself afraid of Him.

Of course there were the "mushy" Christians who would say, "Don't be afraid of God. He just wants to be your best friend." So I came to the point in my life where I said to myself, "If God wants to be my friend, then He needs to show Himself more friendly."

I didn't think Him pushing me around was the best way to win me over. That tactic might have worked as it did when I was in 3rd grade, when the new guy in school, Max, and I got into a shoving match. He gave me a big shove and I gave him a big shove back, causing him to fall to the ground. He picked himself up, we shook hands, and complimented each other for being so strong. We have been best friends ever since. God shoving me to the ground, however, doesn't make me want to get up, dust myself off, and shake His hand for being so strong.

Bible Babble

It was in my teenage years when I decided to pursue God and know Him for myself. There were things I had heard up to that point which made me feel very uncomfortable with His character. I needed to take a closer look. I stared at Him through the book He had been credited for inspiring—the Bible.

If I thought people gave an unfavorable impression of God, the Bible didn't always help clear things up. When we look at the picture of God in the Bible, it is quite subjective at times, similar to my museum experience. I've learned that people can defend almost any belief by a verse here or there. How is this possible? Because the Bible was not written by one person, or even by God. Many different individuals over thousands of years, all who are believed to be inspired by God, contributed their writings on the subject of Him. Only much later was it compiled by early church leaders, who placed the 66 books together in what we now know as the Bible. There were so many human variables involved in this process that many believe the Bible cannot be trusted. Others beg to differ. Although many factors may have contributed to what some now call inconsistencies, I have discovered a thread of unwavering truth that runs from Genesis to Revelation; a truth that pieces together a clear and coherent picture of God.

I was encouraged at the beginning of my journey to realize that God had no problem with me getting to know Him. In fact, He encourages it. God equated the knowledge of Himself with eternal life. Jesus said, "Now this is eternal life: that they may *know you*, the only true God, and Jesus Christ, whom you have sent" (John 17:3, NIV).

I know we've been told not to ask questions and just believe. However, I have learned that God welcomes our questions. They're not an indication of faithlessness, but rather a sincere attempt to strengthen our trust and deepen our understanding. I don't claim to know all the answers, but we can search for them together.

Jesus tells His disciples that He will no longer call them servants, but rather *friends*. His reason for the change? They know Him. Jesus tells them everything, and He wants to tell us everything too.

I know there is a rumor going around that God created us because He wanted to add more servants to His household; more people to obey and worship Him. But is it likely that the only reason we were created is because He wanted to be friendly and meet us face to face? He just happened to be in the neighborhood of His imagination and thought, "Now she would be fun to meet." Is it possible that more than just our Creator, Lord, and Savior, He's *dying* just to be our friend?

A Closer Look

This book is about taking a closer look at the picture of God. It is an accumulation of time spent staring at Him through the Bible and throughout my experiences. It's a sincere attempt to discover who this divine artist truly is by viewing Him in relationship to His artwork—us. How much is His collection worth? What value does He place on it?

Take your time as you look through these pages. Don't allow any symptoms of Attention-Deficit Disorder to get in the way. The longer you stare, the more you will see.

Chapter 1
— The Gospel According to Bart —

"You did not choose me, but I chose you and appointed you to go and bear fruit that will last. ..." John 15:16, NIV

He must have been the quiet kid that used to sit three quarters from the front of the classroom, off to the left. His name was Bart ... No, maybe it was Josh. Or maybe Nathan. Does it really matter what his name was? Whoever he was, it seems he wasn't important enough for you to remember his name. The kid wasn't too smart. He was always last to be picked on a team. His pants were always too tight, too high up on his waist, and too far from his shoes. Before *Napoleon Dynamite* there was Bart ... I mean Nathan ... well, whatever his name was. The only thing memorable about him was that he didn't quite fit in.

I found a disciple of Jesus that fits this same description. Bartholomew was his name—I think. He barely gets a mention in the Bible as one of Jesus' disciples. Scholars believe that he might have been the Nathaniel who is spoken of in the first chapter of John's gospel. Some think his name might have also been Jesus and that the gang referred to him by his last name Bar (son of) -Tholomew. Again, does it really matter? They never got the two Judas' names mixed up in the group.

Peter, James, and John were the distinguished three of the twelve. Not Bart. He never said anything worth remembering or recording. Christian history tells us that Bartholomew was the first to evangelize India, and he even wrote his own gospel record like Matthew and John. But his story never made the press. I guess after one read of *The Gospel According to Bartholomew*, people were begging for a real writer, like Luke, to give them a more compelling version. Poor Bart.

Why did Jesus pick such a quiet guy to be on His team? Why did he pick the guy with the least amount of potential? If he was so unnoticeable, how did Christ notice him? In his book *Messy Spirituality*, Michael Yaconelli writes of an eerily familiar dream:

"I often dream that I am tagging along behind Jesus, longing for him to choose me as one of his disciples. Without warning, he turns around, looks straight into my eyes, and says, "Follow me!" My heart races, and I begin to run toward him when he interrupts with, "Oh, not you; the guy behind you. Sorry."

Ouch!

Middle Child Syndrome

I am a recovering middle child syndromic (yeah, I made it up). I was trapped between my wonderful brother, Bob, who is four years older than me, and my beloved brother, Greg, who is younger by fourteen months. As far back as I can remember I was in the middle. I never experienced the formative years of over-indulgence by my parents because my youngest brother unknowingly robbed me of the glorious opportunity (I told you I was still recovering). Bob was *numero uno*. He spent his first four years being the main attraction, and he took full advantage of it. He had a jump start on every relationship within our extended family. Between Greg the Gift and Bob the Best, I didn't stand a chance. I felt unnoticed, not as important, and a bit dispensable. My sense of worth was low. By the age of five I was fed up with feeling underappreciated. I packed all my belongings in a pillowcase and marched my melodramatic self right out the front door.

Do you ever feel like you don't fit in? You're the oddball in your family, the misfit at school, overlooked at work, and passed over at church. You even play second fiddle in your most intimate relationships. Maybe you don't have middle child syndrome, but you do believe there were greater people before you, and there will be far more spectacular people after you. If the closest people in your life don't even notice you, how is God going to notice you among all the more distinguishable ones? Do you sometimes feel like if you were to ever move away no one would really care?

I am sure there were times when Bart thought of leaving the Formidable Twelve. Surely Saint Mark could take his place. The other disciples might not even notice he was gone. What was worse, Jesus might not even notice.

Part of the Family

With my eyes welled up with tears, I walked slowly up our street with the pillowcase over my back, tightly clenched in my little fist. I knew if I could manage to reach the nearby park, I could find shelter for my weary soul (told you I was melodramatic). My mom told Greg to find our dad so he could find me before I wandered off into the cold, cruel, dark world (OK, I'll stop). I managed to walk 20 sidewalk squares before dad met me at the corner of our street in his car. With a pursed, fat lip, my teary eyes gazed downward as my dad rolled down the window. Bracing myself for an irate interrogation, my dad, however, casually asked me, "What's wrong?" What I was expecting was, "Boy, if you don't get your behind in this car!" But his tenderness and concern came as an unexpected surprise. My defenses were broken and the floodgates opened. I attempted to explain my actions in that *I'm crying but still going to try to talk* voice that only the Holy Spirit could have interpreted. After listening to my babble, and probably doing his best not to laugh at my sincerity, dad asked the million-dollar question for any five-year-old: "Would you like to get some ice cream?"

Now I know almost everyone has a "runaway from home" story. So aren't you supposed to get in trouble for that kind of defection? I expected my dad to punish me immediately. Instead, he treats me. And who was I to argue with him? If he wanted to give his son ice cream, I wasn't going to get in the way. My dad smoothed everything over with a scoop of vanilla. He listened to his five-year-old boy asking in his own way if his little life mattered. Although I have forgotten the words my father shared with me that afternoon, I have never forgotten the way he made me feel. I was assured of my worth. Our family would not be complete without *me*.

The apostle Paul writes:

The eye cannot say to the hand, "I don't need you!" And the head cannot say to the feet, "I don't need you!" On the contrary, those parts of the body that seem to be weaker are indispensable, and the parts that we think are less honorable we treat with special honor. (1 Corinthians 12:21-23, NIV)

I am indispensable! You are indispensable! Even if people think we're not deserving of honor and recognition, God says we are worthy of special treatment. Even if we feel we are of no value, God sees our worth—our indispensability. Even though we all have different gifts, functions, responsibilities and so called disabilities, we are all considered a necessary part of the family. It is so important we understand this truth: each one of us matters. You matter, Bart.

Who Are You?

If there were ever a place and time in earth's history when you didn't want someone to struggle with issues of identity and worth, it would have been in the Garden of Eden. The Tree of Knowledge of Good and Evil was the only access the rebel angel, Satan, had to the newlyweds. Satan, who couldn't handle not being number one in heaven, sought to tempt the humans with the same spirit of discontent and insecurity. As childish as that sounds, most of our conflicts in life revolve around this same issue.

God told Adam and Eve that the day they make the decision to break-up with Him by eating fruit from the Tree of Knowledge, they would "surely die." Satan, through the disguise of a serpent, created doubt in the minds of Earth's first couple by telling them they would not die from eating the fruit. He said the only reason God discouraged them from eating the fruit was to keep them from having the same knowledge as Him—whereby making them gods. Based on the serpent's assertions, the humans felt more knowledge would give them an immediate upgrade in value and worth with a single bite. Wouldn't that be difficult to resist?

So we won't die?

God was just lying to us, trying to keep us from having some fun?

We can be gods?

There is more out there than what we already know?

God must not trust us.

Maybe God is selfish after all.

Maybe He can't be trusted.

"We'll take two pieces of fruit, and put it on our tab, sir."

Amazingly, everything the serpent told them was *seemingly* true. They didn't immediately die after eating the fruit, although they began to die. And God did not want them to become like Him in knowing *both* good and evil. So it was almost true. It just wasn't the entire truth. That is how Satan deceives us all. He mixes in a little bit of error with just the right amount of truth. Or he will present us only truth, but out of its context. Either way, the result is still the same: we are misled. Satan's game is all about deception. If it's not all true and within the right context, then it's all a lie and not of God. Some of us will never know how misled we are until it is too late and our lives are devastated by believing the deception. We must see through the picture of lies.

Opinions, Opinions, Opinions

Similar to Adam and Eve seeing themselves through the eyes of the serpent, most of us see ourselves through the eyes of other people. Their opinions shape how we see ourselves. Negative comments directed at us from our parents, and children ridiculing us through our awkward *Bart* stages in life can still haunt us even now. Outside opinions can influence the clothes we wear, what school we will attend, and even our decision for a marriage partner. Even though we might not like admitting it, we want people's approval. Especially from those we admire. If you liked smoking weed and everyone in the world, including your friends, thought you were a lunatic for smoking weed, how much fun would it really be? Opinions alter our lifestyle.

The decade of the eighties was one convoluted mess of fashion styles, ideologies, and fads for me. I went from wearing a Michael Jackson-like Jheri curl hairdo to wearing Prince inspired lace, to being a *wannabe* skater dude, to thinking I was a hardcore *gangsta'* roughing it on the hard streets of Loma Linda, California. I was a crazy mess. Sometimes I look at pictures from my youth and wonder, "How did my parents let me leave the house looking like that?" It takes many of us a lifetime before we are comfortable in our own skin. I am convinced that at the heart of every delusional thing we do is the intense desire to prove our worth.

We must stop falling for these same old tricks. Every one of us was created to feel good about who we are. No one is born with poor self-esteem. A negative self-image is developed. It is taught and learned. You are feeling great about life until someone comes along and tells you there is something better, bigger, and faster. They say you're too skinny, too fat, too slow, too short, and not cute enough. Then before you know it, like Adam and Eve, you suddenly find yourself dissatisfied—even with perfect happiness! You begin to feel you don't measure up, so you must become smarter, better looking, more aggressive. It's all an illusion. Marketing strategists understand this desire to become something other than what we are, and continue to create false needs and more empty desires through advertising, so that we will want to readily purchase their products.

Satan created a desire in the first couple that was never there before: *you should be like God.* Adam and Eve already thought they were like God because they had been created in His image and likeness (Genesis 1:27). So when the serpent said they really weren't like God, then they desired to be. What they failed to realize, though, is that they were already like Him. They were His image! Adam and Eve had need of nothing. They already had what they were tempted to pursue—God-*likeness.*

God has "given us everything we need for life and godliness through our knowledge of Him who called us by his own glory and goodness" (2 Peter 1:3, NIV). Although people's opinions usually impact our lives, God would like His opinion to have the greatest impact.

Image Consultant

Even Jesus needed a reminder of who He was before embarking on Mission Impossible. If there were anyone in history who should have struggled with self-image issues, it was Jesus. He went from Creator to conceived. From King to servant. And when you factor in that Jesus was scheduled for a 40 day stretch of bad sleep, no food, no cell phone reception, and testing from His rival Satan in a hot wilderness, anyone would have begun to doubt their identity. So before His trip into the desert, the Father publicly reminded Jesus of His no-longer-secret identity. *This is my Son. I love Him so much. I'm very proud of Him* (Mark 1:10-11).

At the end of His 40 days in the wilderness, Jesus was confronted by His enemy. By beginning each temptation with, "*If* you are the Son of God," Satan severely challenged Jesus' identity; but Jesus knew He could not give in. He had to trust what His Father said about Him 40 days prior. Jesus responds to Satan's temptation with this declaration: "Man does not live by bread alone, but by the words that come from the mouth of God" (Matthew 4:4). We need to live confidently by those same words.

I have found that the only way to successfully fight against a poor self-image is to know who we are, and to whom we belong. Even though they were created in the image of God, Adam and Eve became confused about their identity. We have the same confusion. So just in case you don't know, or you forgot who you are, allow me to remind you. Your breath came from God. Your soul is connected with His. You are beloved, forever, and tremendously adored by God. He loves you more than life itself. You are His precious girl. You are His baby boy. Hollywood might say you need a tummy tuck, an eyebrow lift, a few implants here and there, to gain 15 more pounds of muscle or lose 15 more pounds of fat. However, your Father formed you in your mother's womb for His own viewing pleasure and not for the subscribers of *Cosmopolitan Magazine*. Listen to the opinion of the Expert who is perfect, rather than the professed experts who change their minds about what perfection looks like from month to month. Listen to the One who has an eye for beauty. God thinks you are pretty special, and He came a long way just to let you know. Similar to my father, He jumped in His car and drove all the way from heaven to meet us at the corner of planet Earth. So let's trade in our poor self-image for the image God sees in us—His image.

> *Your worth does not come from your body, your mind, your work, what you produce, what you put out, how much money you make. Your worth does not come from whether or not you have a man [or woman]. Your worth does not come from whether or not men [or women] notice you. You have inestimable worth that comes from your Creator. You will continue to be tempted in a thousand different ways not to believe this. The temptation will be to go searching for your worth and validity from places other than your Creator.* —Rob Bell

A Part of the Team

Remember, God pursued you. He called you. God has a great eye for talent and He chose you. In the end, even if you are the last player off the bench, you get the same trophy as Kobe Bryant and Shaquille O'Neal. Do you remember Bobby Hansen? Most people don't. But he is the guy wearing an NBA championship ring from a Michael Jordan-led Chicago Bulls team that won it all in 1992. Even though you have no stats next to your name on the game sheet, you can still say you are a part of the team. In the end, you will receive a championship crown.

Even if no one else can get your name right, God knows your name. So what if he was picked 7th, 10th, or even last to be on the team? The point is that Bartholomew was picked. Maybe he didn't have the fiery passion of Peter or the thunderous preaching skills of James and John.

Maybe he wasn't as shrewd as Judas or as intellectual as Thomas. All we really know about Bart is that he was there, and was worth mentioning. You might think you are an afterthought, but God says you are a forethought—*I knew you before you were born* (Jeremiah 1:5). God "chose us in him before the creation of the world … to be adopted as his sons [and daughters] in Jesus Christ" (Ephesians 1:4-5, NIV). God sees the big picture, and you are in it.

King of the Hill

The name Bartholomew means "hill" in Hebrew. He didn't even have the privilege of being named after a great mountain. No worries though, for I remember God doing something special on a hill a couple thousand years ago. Christian tradition tells us that after a life full of service, which barely gets a mention, Bartholomew becomes a martyr. Don't be too sad about the way things ended here on earth for Bart. Word has it that one of the twelve foundations, which help support the "New Jerusalem," has his name on it (Revelation 21:14). Maybe when we all get there we'll finally learn his real name. And maybe, just maybe, we can hear *The Gospel According to Bartholomew*, personally.

p.s. God has your name etched in His heart. Jesus has it permanently tattooed all over His back and carved into His hands. His family would not be complete without you. He wants you. He chose you. He pursued you. You matter.

Chapter 2
—— When Good Isn't Good Enough ——

"I am the true vine, and my Father is the gardener. He cuts off every branch in me that bears no fruit, while every branch that does bear fruit he prunes so that it will be even more fruitful." John 15:1-2, NIV

He was a self-made man; distinguished, rich, powerful, and young. Everything he wanted, he acquired. Every pursuit and goal was achieved. For a man who approaches his everyday life in this manner, why should he approach eternal life any differently? Salvation was just another notch on his belt. That would soon change after a brief business meeting with heaven's Broker. The savvy businessman treats this encounter with Jesus like any other transaction—he starts off with flattery. "Good teacher. May I please have a word with you? What must I do to receive eternal life?" That is a loaded question. In fact, that might be the single most important question every person asks. Jesus, sensing where the young man is going with this, attempts to redirect the conversation. "Why do you call me good? Don't you know there is only One who is good?" (Matthew 19:17, NIV).

How much easier would life be if we could just believe this statement? No more self-abuse. No more kicking ourselves when we are down. No more guilt-ridden nights which keep us awake. Just the simple acknowledgement that God is good and we are not. Doesn't that take the load off your back? Not for this rich dude. He wants the burden. He is up for the task and Jesus lets him have it. *"Obey all the commandments if you want eternal life."*

"Which ones?" the rich guy asks.

"Do not murder, do not steal, do not commit adultery, do not tell lies about others, honor your parents, love your neighbor as you love yourself. ... "

"Pardon me teacher, but let me make this easier on you. Since I have obeyed these commandments you speak of, why don't you just tell me what else I need to do. I mean, am I perfect, or what?"

"If you want to be perfect, sell all of your possessions, then give that money to the poor and you will have treasures in heaven. Then, I want you to follow me" (Matthew 19:17-21).

Did you hear that? Everything! Let's see here ... empty the bank account, sell the house, the cars, and oh yeah, you might even have to say good-bye to your love-life. You might have nothing left on earth. *Follow me.* It requires that you forget about what pleases you. And just so you know, there will be a cross you'll have to carry (Matthew 16:24).

What kind of person would take Christ up on that offer? There is just too much sacrifice in His business proposal. I lose too much of myself in His merger of corporations—or should I say *hostile takeover?* Yeah, maybe the health benefits and the life insurance policy are great, but why would God demand so much of me? I can't blame the young guy for his next move. He sadly went away. He wasn't a bad guy, just not a *perfect* guy. I guess being good isn't good enough.

Jesus then says it is easier for a camel to go through the "eye of a needle than for a rich man to enter the kingdom of God" (Matthew 19:24, NIV). In laymen's terms, that basically means it's impossible. The disciples felt the same way. Astonished, they asked, "Who then can be saved?" (Matthew 19:25).

We all have some form of wealth in our lives. It can be our home, car, job, relationships, collectibles—things we just don't want to give up for God. And Jesus says it is impossible for people like us to make it into heaven. Anybody ready to sign on the dotted line? The problem is that it's just too difficult to meet God's standards. The bar has been set too high.

Big Loser

One of the most exciting times in my life occurred when I played for my college basketball team during my sophomore year. My chest would swell up with pride when I walked off the team bus to play our games. Home games were even more exciting because I had the opportunity to play in front of friends and classmates. I was having so much fun! I ate, drank, and slept basketball. I would watch basketball videos and play basketball video games with my friend and teammate,

William. We would play from evening until the early hours of morning. You would have thought we were paying all that money for college to attend some basketball camp rather than for a higher education. Unfortunately, my joy and enthusiasm came to a crashing halt when I received my report card for the first quarter. My G.P.A. was a whopping 1.7! It needed to be a 2.0 to maintain eligibility to play. I was so embarrassed. I wasn't even allowed to take a picture with the team for the yearbook. I felt like the biggest failure on campus. I went from making the team to being kicked off.

Being kicked off the roster was also my worst fear when it came to my relationship with God. He would get me all excited by choosing me. Then, after some time, I would realize how difficult it was to stay on the team. I felt it was impossible to maintain the necessary G.P.A. with God. He was demanding perfection. I needed a 4.0. I couldn't just get by with being an average 2.3 follower. Even the 3.9 students, like the rich guy, weren't making it. It seemed impossible! Why is doing the right thing so difficult all the time? No one can be perfect!

Rockers

My mom repeatedly told my brothers and I not to throw rocks. One day Greg, who I blame 100% for the whole fiasco, egged me on saying, "I bet you can't throw a rock farther than me." I am older than him, and presumably stronger, so I couldn't let this blatant disregard of my superiority go unchallenged. We were standing at the furthest edge of the backyard when my six-year-old brother cleared the roof of our house with a perfectly thrown rock that would have made King David proud. It was now my duty to outmatch him. But who was I kidding? Even though I was stronger, I could throw about as well as Winnie the Pooh. I wound my arm and threw it so high and far that I couldn't even see it in the air. My attempt was a good one ... if I were aiming for the window of my brother's bedroom. The noise of the crashing glass was so loud that I knew my mom must have heard it. I ran as fast as I could to be in the house by the time she figured out what had caused the noise. In the four seconds it took me to arrive at the sliding glass door, I had already come up with the real stone-throwing culprits— our neighbors! It was all for naught when I saw her waiting for me at the door. Oh boy, I knew I was going to get it. To add insult to injury, she made me wait in the room with the broken glass as she carefully selected the instrument of ... well, you get the picture.

I was clearly told what not to do. I disobeyed. According to mom, I deserved the punishment. How many of us view God's justice this way? God clearly and repeatedly tells us what to do, or not to do, but we just can't seem to follow instructions. It's like we see this bright red button that reads "Do Not Touch" and instead of being a deterrent, we consider it an invitation to push it. As Paul confessed, "I want to do what is right, but I can't. I want to do what is good, but I don't. I don't want to do what is wrong, but I do it anyway" (Romans 7:18-19, NLT). This is quite a confession from the man who almost single-handedly spread the Christian faith throughout the then-known world.

Why are we like this? Why is it so difficult to be obedient? In short, we are a messed-up people. The Bible calls this condition sin. The word *sin* literally means *to miss the mark*. God is 4.0, and sin is 3.9. It can be a small fraction of a difference from God's perfect plan, or a titanic change from His proposed course. If it deters, distracts, or disables you from accepting God's ideal for your life, it is sin. That is our predicament. We are sinners. We are experts at missing the mark. Our hearts are incredibly selfish. We are born bent towards doing wrong. We don't even do *good* things for the right reasons. We just don't have our stuff together and I don't understand it, but I hear there is someone who does.

Our Condition

A crowd of real rock-throwing experts surrounded a woman caught in the act of adultery. They asked Jesus what they should do with such a sinner. Jesus, knowing fully that the Law condemned such a person to death by stoning, responded with, "If any of you have never sinned, then go ahead and throw the first stone at her" (John 8:7, CEV). We have all sinned. None of us could have thrown a rock at her, but what about the Rock of Ages Himself? He is perfect. He could have loaded up the fold of His robe with rocks and just pegged this woman from every angle. So why didn't Jesus peg her?

It appears that God is not nearly as hard on us as we are on ourselves. He understands the sin problem. He knows the unfair disadvantages in our life. He knows that you had no decision in being born on this planet. God sees your abusive parents, or lack of parents. He knows the path of circumstances that led you to drug addiction. Negative influences can be found in your choice of music and on television. Even your poverty or wealth has contributed to your situation. He cannot blame you for being infected with this deadly virus of disobedience. Adam and Eve passed on the first sexually transmitted disease called "sin" (Romans 5:12). As a result, everyone after them had a propensity for disobeying God. Jesus, understanding our problem, decided to do something about it. He injected the cure from His veins into ours. The Bible calls this *grace*. Paul cries out, "What a miserable person I am. Who will rescue me from this body that is doomed to die? Thank God! Jesus Christ will rescue me" (Romans 7:24-25, CEV).

Who's to Blame?

I have to admit that I felt it was God's duty to clean up the sin problem since I believed He was responsible for creating the situation. But I discovered that God is no more responsible for sin than my parents are if I crashed their car. Did my parents know I had the potential to drive the car recklessly when they let me borrow it? Yeah, but I can't blame them for the accident just because they trusted me with some responsibility. Couples have babies all the time, fully knowing that their child is going to grow up into an adult with the capacity to completely reject them if they so choose. Also knowing the risks associated with having children, such as Sudden Infant Death Syndrome (SIDS), mental and physical disabilities, and the possibility of developing future addictions, couples still take the risk of having children.

God created intelligent human beings in His *likeness*. Great were the risks and potential for us to choose a different way because He endowed us with the freedom of choice. Fish cannot choose like you and I. Although they are living creatures, they do not have our cognitive reasoning abilities. Same with cows. Dogs can make you feel good about coming home from work, but you know they would respond that way to anyone who fed them. Humans are a whole other kind of creature. Like animals, we can be quite instinctual, but our ability to reason and create is an example of our having been created in the image of God. But with the decision to create us in His image, God took a huge risk. A cat could never create a nuclear weapon, but with humans, almost nothing is impossible (Gen 11:6).

God was willing to be vulnerable and take the risk of rejection from beings that were like Him. That is why we can be hurt far worse by rejection from a fellow human being than we can from a pet canary. There is risk in getting married. Although there is immense joy in finding the person who will love you unconditionally, you equally run the risk of that special someone eventually hating every fiber of your existence. So what do you do? Marry something not like you? You can marry a tree—tall, sturdy, dependable. No risk there. Neither is there much of a chance for any meaningful conversation, or opportunity to be authentically loved in return. You can marry the squirrel in the tree. She wouldn't require you to spend a lot of money on her. A few acorns would satisfy, and you could count on her to be faithful until the end. But then again, you are still missing the component of emotional and cognitive reflection. Sure, the squirrel gives you a few laughs because she's cute, but not because she has a great sense of humor. You can marry someone like you, "bone of [your] bone and flesh of [your] flesh" (Genesis 2:23, NIV). It will be risky, but it just might be worth it.

God was attracted to the idea of being in a consensual, loving relationship with humanity. He could have sheltered them from evil and pretended it didn't exist, but that would not have shown integrity and transparency. Adam and Eve deserved, at the very least, a choice. So God trusted them in the garden of paradise; with the keys to the vehicle. He trusted them with the Tree of Knowledge of Good and Evil in the heavily trafficked intersection of the garden. The tree was *smack dab* in the middle of Eden. God did not hide it in a corner and cover it with cobwebs. He placed it right next to the remote for the TV. God could have placed an electric fence around the tree, but that would not have shown trust in His new creation. God could not entertain a relationship with His new companions that was not based on free will. Love can only be genuine in freedom; even if that same freedom meant that He could end up losing us.

Unfortunately, the couple chose a different path. They wrecked the car. And as a result sin entered the world. On the day Adam and Eve sinned, God came to visit His companions. On this occasion, they were nowhere to be found. They were hiding. They were lost. So what was God to do? He couldn't just leave them alone to die. He wanted to do something about it. He came to the rescue.

Holding Your Breath

When I was eight, we welcomed a new addition into our family. I remember when my little bro', Rafik, finally made it out of diapers and was potty-trained. It was a time of celebration until my brothers and I realized that although Rafik could now make it to the toilet, he wasn't quite an expert with using toilet paper. You can imagine how many arguments my brothers and I had about whose turn it was to assist Rafik with "going to the potty." It's one thing to clean up your own mess, it's another thing to clean up after someone else. When it was my turn, I would hold my breath and walk into the bathroom. Please don't give me any medals of honor because somebody had to do it. Rafik couldn't, so I came through for the little stinker.

God knew we couldn't clean ourselves, so He came through for us. Unlike when Satan and his angelic followers sinned in heaven with a perfect knowledge of God, we were still toddlers, barely potty-trained. So God had compassion on us. He chose to clean up a mess He didn't make. God wanted to give us more opportunities to get to know Him better. He walked into our earth, closed the door behind Him, and didn't even hold His breath. If we could have cleaned up our own mess, His services would not have been needed. Remember, God understands why we are a disobedient, selfish, and sinful people. He knows we didn't choose to be born into this degenerative state. His sympathy for our situation was the reason He came to rescue us. If He didn't understand, He wouldn't have come.

I remember watching soap operas with my mom, and every now and then they would change actors for a particular character. A God-like voice would announce the change, "The part of Erica Steel will now be played by Barbara Stevens." That is very similar to how God changed actors in the middle of the soap *As the World Turns*: "The character of Adam will now be played by Jesus" (Romans 5:12-19). Adam's sin plummeted the whole world into a spiraling death trap. Now, after changing actors, the new Adam, Jesus, changes mankind's course with His righteous and gracious act. Jesus read for the sinner's part—which led to death. He took Adam's place. He took our place. God knows life can be unfair, and He did His best to tip the scale in our favor.

He asks the woman caught in adultery, "Where are those who were accusing you?" Her head had been buried in the dirt in fear and shame. She never even saw the crowd clear out, leaving their rocks behind. Jesus lifts her chin up gently with His finger, and with tears in His eyes says to her and us, "Neither do I condemn you" (John 8:10-11, NIV).

All Things are Possible

After Jesus' speech about the camel and the needle, the disciples ask, "Teacher, who then can be saved?" Jesus smiles at them and gives them the gospel message. "For man it is impossible, but with God *all* things are possible" (Matthew 19:26, NIV). Wow! I was just feeling as lost as that rich, young guy; as desperate as the adulterer. I felt like the cost to go to heaven was too high, and I wasn't good enough. And I was right. I'm not good enough, but Jesus is. It does cost too much, but He willingly paid for it.

I wish I knew which one of the disciples ran to catch up with the rich guy to let him know it was not over yet—it was *not* impossible. Jesus told this parable about the camel and the needle not to discourage rich people from entering into the kingdom, but to encourage them on how they could enter the kingdom. A wealthy man, or a poor one for that matter, cannot attain the riches of eternal life without the only *One Who is Good*. We are far too selfish, vain, and lazy to travel the required path to God's kingdom by ourselves. We need help. We need a Teacher. We need a Savior. How can anyone miss out on heaven when God makes it so accessible through His generosity, love, and grace? He does not place the burden of perfection on us. He placed it firmly on the back of someone He could trust. He placed the burden on His Son, and Jesus carried it to a place called Calvary. He was the only one who could score the 4.0 G.P.A. He was the only one who was perfect. He was the only One good enough.

p.s. I guess you can say the bar was set high. I am just relieved that Christ was willing not only to reach it, but to stretch out his hands across the bar and give His life for us.

Chapter 3
—— Angry with God ——

"They hated me without reason." John 15:25, NIV

Has anyone whom you've looked up to let you down? It can be quite devastating. Have you ever let someone down who looked up to you? Toward the end of my senior year in high school, I landed my first job. It was given to me based on a strong referral from one of the business' employees, who just happened to be one of my best friends. I had such a strong sense of achievement when I put on my uniform for the first time. No one would ever look at me the same way. I felt as if I were two feet taller ... and actually, I was two feet taller. I was Chuck E. Cheese. Next to Mickey Mouse, I was the most recognized rodent among children.

One day I was doing a little song and dance for two birthday parties taking place simultaneously. As I ran from one table to another, one of the birthday boys decided to run up and give me a hug during my routine. Unfortunately, I didn't have great visibility under Chuck's huge head. I could only see through an opening in the mouth, so when I turned around to run back to the other table to finish the birthday song, my leg hit something—hard. I looked through the hole of the mouth to see the birthday boy fly across the room in slow motion saying, "Chuuuck Eeeeee, noooooooooo!" His family quickly surrounded him to check if he was hurt. I tried to help, but who was I kidding? I was a six-foot, mute rat in overalls who had just kicked a child across the room. I felt awful. I went from being the friend that all the children would share their secrets with, to being just a big bully. The boy wanted me to be a part of his milestone event, and what did I do? Let him down. Literally.

Ok, I know my Chuck E. Cheese incident humorously pales in comparison to some of your heart-wrenching stories of disappointment. You cheated someone or cheated on them. They lied to you or about you. It's extremely difficult to work through our feelings of disappointment and hurt when someone lets us down, or vice versa.

In the gospels, Jesus is always portrayed as a hero with perfect timing. The phrase "He might not be there when you need Him, but He's always on time" never made much sense to me. I used to say "Amen" anyway because it sounded deep and profound. But how can He be there on time when He is not there when I need Him? I have a feeling that Mary and Martha didn't say "Amen" when they heard that sound bite in church three days after their brother Lazarus died. Word had been sent to Jesus that Lazarus, His good friend, was deathly ill. Jesus shot back an email, "This sickness will not end in death. No, it is for God's glory so that God's Son may be glorified through it" (John 11:4, NIV). "Cool," the sisters said, until after a few days Lazarus rolled over and died. Talk about a letdown! Jesus assures them their brother will not die, and a few days later he looks like the biggest liar. Has God ever looked like a liar to you? Honestly, how many times have you felt like He has let you down? How many times have you wanted to tell Him to His face that you don't believe Him anymore? I know it's hard to say that to God, but a lot of us have felt that way.

Sitting on [the] Job

One of the most honest and straightforward takes on God is found in the book of Job. Many people love to quote this book in the Bible as the uniform way to respond to life's hardships. Job appears to be an innocent bystander of God and Satan's wager. Old Pitchfork shows up late for one of heaven's board meetings as the representative from planet Earth. God asks where he has been, and Satan replies, "Just walking back and forth on earth."

"Have you noticed my friend Job?" God inquires. "Is there anyone on earth who does more good?"

Satan shoots back, "He's only good because you favor him. If you remove your protection and let me have my way with him, he'll curse you to your face."

"Deal. But you cannot harm his body."

Job endures a whirlwind of unimaginable loss. Within a matter of 30 seconds he hears that he has lost his family, his business, and his retirement savings (Job 1:13-19). And what was his response to this catastrophe?

He tore his clothes and shaved his head because of his great sorrow. He knelt on the ground, then worshiped God and said: "We bring nothing at birth; we take nothing with us at death. The LORD alone gives and takes. Praise the name of the LORD!" In spite of everything, Job did not sin or accuse God of doing wrong. (Job 1:20-22, NIV)

Amazing response from Job! Even more amazing, there were more attacks to come. At the very next board meeting, Satan assures God that if he is allowed to harm Job's body, he will surely curse God to His face. God consents and Satan makes Job's body break out with painful, puss oozing sores from head to toe. His wife asked, "Why do you still trust God? Why don't you curse him and die?" Job replied, "Don't talk crazy! If we accept blessings from God, we must accept trouble as well." In all that happened, Job never once said anything against God (Job 2:9-10).

In light of Job's incredible resolve, most Christians are encouraged to take Job's attitude towards life's difficult and painful trials—illness, infidelity, divorce, or death of a loved one. Just respond like Job. Maybe God is bragging about you in heaven. Maybe He's testing you. Doesn't that make you feel better? Not me. And guess what? Not even Job. You see, Job is only calm for the first two chapters of the book. The book is 42 chapters long! In chapter three, Job begins to curse. Not God, but the day he was born. "Blot out the day of my birth and the night when my parents created a son. Forget about that day, cover it with darkness" (Job 3:3-4, CEV).

As the book continues, Job becomes more aggressive and accusatory with God. Here are a few angry text messages he sent to both his friends and God:

Why is life so hard? Why do we suffer? ... God has made my days drag on and my nights miserable. ... I beg you, God, don't forget! My life is just a breath, and trouble lies ahead. ... And so, I cry out to you in agony and distress. ... I'd rather choke to death than live in this body. Leave me alone and let me die; my life has no meaning. What makes you so concerned about us humans? Why do you test us from sunrise to sunset? Won't you look away just long enough for me to swallow? Why do you watch us so closely? What's it to you, if I sin? Why am I your target and such a heavy burden? Why do you refuse to forgive?" (Job 7:1, 3, 7, 11, 15-20, CEV)

Did Job experience a lapse in judgment? You cannot accuse God of using you for target practice, can you? Just when I thought Job was done venting, he takes it to whole 'nother level.

Even though I am innocent, I can only beg for mercy. And if God came into court when I called him, he would not hear my case. He would strike me with a storm and increase my injuries for no reason at all. Before I could get my breath, my miseries would multiply. God is much stronger than I am, and who would call me into court to give me justice? Even if I were innocent, God would prove me wrong. I am not guilty, but I no longer care what happens to me. What difference does it make? God destroys the innocent along with the guilty. When a good person dies a sudden death, God sits back and laughs. And who else but God blindfolds the judges, then lets the wicked take over the earth? My life is speeding by, without a hope of happiness. Each day passes swifter than a sailing ship or an eagle swooping down. Sometimes I try to be cheerful and to stop complaining, but my sufferings frighten me, because I know that God still considers me guilty. So what's the use of trying to prove my innocence? Even if I washed myself with the strongest soap, God would throw me into a pit of stinking slime, leaving me disgusting to my clothes. God isn't a mere human like me. I can't put him on trial. Who could possibly judge between the two of us? Can someone snatch away the stick God carries to frighten me? Then I could speak up without fear of him, but for now, I cannot speak. (Job 9:14-35, CEV)

Why didn't anyone want to quote these verses? Will the real Job please stand up? I know most of you have never sent such angry text messages to God. I also know you have them saved as drafts, just in case. I remember reading these texts for the first time and being scared for Job. I thought God was going to strike him down with lightning for the things he was saying. He blinds all the judges? He wouldn't even show up to court if you had a dispute with Him? God uses us for target practice? He laughs when innocent people die? You don't just say those things about God and live. And the most disturbing moments during Job's tirade are when God appears content to remain silent. Job has lost everything, including his mind, and God says nothing.

Unfriendly Skies

I was on my computer typing away at a blistering fourteen words per minute. There was a soft engine hum throughout the cabin as passengers were readjusting themselves, attempting to remain comfy during the long flight home. The couple behind me had chosen the in-flight movie, while the two teenage boys in front of me were busy listening to their iPods. An older woman occupied the seat next to mine, reading a novel warmly lit by her assigned overhead lamp.

I was traveling back to Oakland, California from a New York speaking engagement. I have made these flights a hundred times in my life, but this time proved to be particularly different from the rest. As I continued to type away, the plane suddenly began to shake violently. I'd experienced turbulence before, so this was nothing new. The captain usually attempted to soothe our fears by telling the passengers to fasten their seatbelts while we experienced a little "bumpy air." However, this bumpiness felt more like we were crashing into the clouds. Being a pastor, I felt pressure to play it cool. The lady next to me kept gasping with each free-fall of the plane. Me? Still halfway cool. At least I was until the captain said the unthinkable—nothing! We went through an hour of non-stop "bumpy air", and the captain said nothing! Before the turbulence, we couldn't shut him up. He would unnecessarily inform us that we were 33, 000 feet in the air. Who cared? He gave us all the names of our flight attendants as if we were going to send them thank you cards. Some lake was to the left and a cluster of mountains to the right, but none of that mattered. We were all feeling the fear of death, and yet the captain said nothing—not one word. How cruel! How insensitive! Where was that velvety voice when you needed it? We couldn't keep him quiet in the beginning, and then he's nowhere to be heard. His silence was excruciating. How could the captain keep quiet at a time like this? Was he scared too? Had he lost control?

Have you ever felt that God was silent when you needed Him to speak up? Did you feel He avoided you when you needed Him the most? How could God just stand by and say nothing during your most turbulent trials in life? Why didn't He speak to Job? Why hadn't Jesus spoken to Lazarus' sisters since their brother's death?

Using the "If" Word

Apparently, Jesus' silence does not last forever because He finally decides to show His face. When Martha heard that Jesus was on His way to visit them, she ran out of the house to meet Him. The first words out of her mouth upon seeing Jesus were, "Lord, *if* you had only been here sooner, my brother would still be alive" (John 11:21, NIV). In other words, it's *your* fault that my brother is dead! It is easy to blame God when we know He has the power to prevent every catastrophe and disaster from happening. OK, so maybe He didn't directly harm Job and his family, but wasn't God indirectly responsible? Wasn't Jesus indirectly at fault for the death of Lazarus? Lord, *if!*

- *If* only you answered my prayers the way I wanted.
- *If* only you prevented me from being assigned to the war.
- *If* only you didn't allow my spouse to be unfaithful.
- *If* only you had protected my son from being hit by that drunken driver.

When we use the *If* word with God, it is our passive-aggressive way of saying, "You are not doing your job. You failed me. It's all your fault." Isn't that what Job is saying? Isn't that what Martha is implying? Isn't that the way you feel?

The best part of this story, so far, is that God allows them to express their frustration. He doesn't tell them to watch their mouths. He just sits there and takes it. What does this tell us about our God? We can tell Him anything. Even when we don't like Him, despise Him, are bored with Him, don't trust Him, or think He's crazy; we can still tell Him, and He will listen.

Laughing at God

One of the stories that inspired me to see past God's silence and give Him a closer look is found in the life of Abraham. One day, God decided to visit Abraham's home. As custom dictated, Abe offered his guest food and something to drink. After eating, they sat and talked about life and the future. God reminded Abraham that He will be blessed with a child and his descendants will be as many as the stars in the sky. Now Abe has heard this speech before. Almost 25 years prior, when he was in his seventies. He is now 99 years old, and his wife, Sarah, is 89. She has never been pregnant in her life. When she overhears God reminding Abraham of His promise, she laughs to herself asking, "Do our parts still work?" God then stops in mid-sentence, turns towards the tent where Sarah is washing dishes and asks, "Why did Sarah just laugh at what I said?" Embarrassed and afraid, Sarah runs out of the tent and tells God, "I didn't laugh!"

You have to understand that when I first read this story I thought Sarah was a goner. I mean, who laughs at God and lives? She increased the likelihood of being incinerated by lying to His face. I can just see God's eyes lighting up with fire. And God's response to the laughing and lying? "Yes, you did laugh" (Genesis 18:1-15, NIV).

I was about 17-years-old when I first read this story, and I started cracking up. This was the first time I had ever laughed after reading something from the Bible. I expected such a different response from the Alpha and Omega. "Yes, you did laugh." That's all you're going to say? No spanking or time-out? Just a simple grin and acknowledgement? Maybe I really didn't know God after all.

God understands our anger and frustration. He understands our doubt and cynicism. He understands when it is directed at Him. He knows why you think He has let you down. He understands our perspective. He knows why you use the *if* word. That is why He allows us to laugh at Him. He even allows us to curse Him, beat Him, and hang Him on a cross.

Silent Treatment

God's silence is empathetic. It should not communicate indifference, but rather trust. He trusts you with His silence. There is something to be learned in the quietude that we could not learn otherwise. God chooses to be a good listener when no amount of explaining will do. If all it would take were an explanation and all our troubles would go away, God would have a list of explanations as far as the eye could see. However, God does something far greater. Instead of explaining the situation, He becomes the situation. He owns it for himself. He remains silent until He can no longer hold back. He keeps silent until He breaks the stillness of the night with a baby's cry in a Bethlehem stable.

p.s. Ready or not, here He comes.

Chapter 4

— Seeing Clearly —

"If the world hates you, keep in mind that
it hated me first." John 15:18, NIV

My brother, Greg, went through a really nerdy stage in his life. From the clothes he wore to the company he kept. Greg was one of the few people I knew who actually wanted to wear glasses to dress up his nerdy-ness. These were during the days when no pair of glasses looked cool. He coerced my grandparents into taking him to an optometrist so he could be fitted to be Mr. Four-Eyes. When he came back from the doctor, he looked like a freak. I told him, "You just wanted glasses. You don't even need them!" Greg did his best to assure me that they were necessary and now he could see things clearly. He started pointing to distant objects in the room that he could now see in pristine detail.

The one item that caught my attention was the digital clock on the VCR, which was about ten feet from us. He said, "I can even see what time it is from here." I looked at the VCR and was unable to make out the time, so I shot back, "You're not supposed to see the time from here." Or should you? My curiosity finally got the best of me and I asked Greg for his glasses. When I put those glasses on, I was ushered into a world of magical delight. I saw things I had never seen before. Everything seemed to jump out at me. All the colors were so vivid. The world was beautiful. I then begged my grandparents to make another appointment with the optometrist. I soon discovered that my eyesight was worse than Greg's. The ride home from the optometrist's office with my new glasses was a wonderland of visual delicacies—the sharp details of the rolling hills, the deep blue of the sky, and the sparkling sun drops that shimmered on everything my eyes could see. The entire way back I kept removing and replacing my glasses on my nose so I could see the difference. It was so exciting. Life is radically different when you can see clearly.

Real Life

Wanting to see more clearly why Christ had not healed her brother, Martha cries, "Lord, *if* you had only come sooner." Jesus places His hand on her shoulder and assures her that her brother *will* rise again. Shaking her head as if in disbelief, and unable to look Jesus in the eye, she mumbles, "I know he will on the resurrection day" (John 11:21-24). Martha was educated in the study of eschatology. Jesus' triumphant Second Coming brought her no relief from the grief. It was too distant. Too intangible. Almost surreal. It wasn't helpful. It was similar to how I felt on my choppy flight, after all the turbulence, and we had begun our descent. The captain finally spoke up and apologized for the rough ride. He then went on to explain how he did his best to find smoother air but was unsuccessful. I'm sorry, but the captain's explanation wasn't good enough. It came at the end of the flight! I needed to know he was on top of his job earlier.

Jesus attempting to explain things to Martha is the same as when people say God will explain everything to us when we get to heaven. What if I don't like His explanation in the end? I don't want clarification then, I want it now. I need God to help me understand life's dilemmas while it is still relevant. I need to be equipped for the present battle; not afterwards when I'm cleaning my wounds and drying my tears.

Jesus, understanding this need, embraces Martha. As she continues to sob in His arms, He tells her, "I am the resurrection and the life. Those who believe in me will live, even though they die; and whoever lives and believes in me will never die" (John 11:25, NIV). What a power packed statement! Jesus basically tells Martha that He is the origin of life. The epicenter of life. In the beginning He was with God and He was God. Through Him *all* things were created (John 1:1-4). Jesus is divinity clothed in humanity. Martha shared her concerns with Jesus, and He simply reminded her of who He was.

God Is On the Job

It looks like Job could use a reminder of who God is. After Job and his friends are finished with their theological discourse, it was time for God to respond. The captain of the plane was ready to speak. Who better to set the record straight about His job performance than God Himself? He's going to answer all the Marthas and Jobs out there. He is going to take us to the optometrist.

Can you answer the questions I ask? How did I lay the foundation for the earth? Were you there? ... Job, have you ever walked on the ocean floor? ... And how large is the earth? Tell me, if you know! Where is the home of light, and where does darkness live? Can you lead them home? I'm certain you must be able to, since you were already born when I created everything *(a little divine sarcasm)*. ... Who is the father of the dew and of the rain? Who gives birth to the sleet and the frost that fall in winter, when streams and lakes freeze solid as a rock? Can you arrange stars? Can you arrange stars in groups such as Orion and the Pleiades? Do you control the stars or set in place the Big Dipper and the Little Dipper? Do you know the laws that govern the heavens, and can you make them rule the earth? Can you order the clouds to send a downpour, or will lightning flash at your command? (Job 38:3-4, 16, 18-21, 28-35, CEV)

Just as you think God is about to finish, He speaks of His intimate knowledge of hippos, bears, deer, goats, lions, oxen, horses, hawks, and some scary Godzilla-like creature named Leviathan. Job tries to backtrack and say he spoke too soon. However, the Creator commands him to man-up and continue the divine pop quiz. When God is finished, Job is left with this one prevailing thought: *"There are a lot of things I don't know."*

Perfect Will vs. Permissive Will

For a second we almost fooled ourselves. Forget about the fear of being kicked off of God's team; we were ready to have Him fired as the coach. We thought all the questions we were hurling at God were making Him look less and less competent as President of the Universe. We actually thought we could sway a few votes in our direction. God was about to be impeached from office and one of us would be elected as the new Supreme Ruler. I can just hear the acceptance speech: "And as your newly elected Lord, I will promise you no more wars, no more natural disasters, no more suffering, and no more death! Life will be perfect! Vote for me!" If I weren't so sure of our pure motives, I would think we were prepared to run a dictatorship, forcing everyone to comply with our new Utopian Society.

God could easily push a button and force everyone to comply as well, but that would take away the fundamental privilege of our humanity—free will. God didn't build robots. He created human beings in His own image.

God's *perfect will* is that we all obey His commandments and experience His kingdom right now. He wishes the whole world would trust Him and His principles. We would have heaven here on earth if only we listened to God. There would be no world hunger, HIV, or any need for law enforcement officers. There would be no crime of any sort, anywhere. Everyone would choose to be loving, kind, and giving. Homelessness would not exist if we would simply respond favorably to God's perfect will for our lives.

God's *permissive will*, however, allows us to be our stubborn old selves. Our continual poor and selfish decisions are the reason the world is in its current condition. It's a mess because God refuses to take away our freedom of choice. He could rid the world of all the rapists, murderers, and drug addicts; but that would mean He would have to be consistent with all the divine law-breakers—including you. No more illicit sexual relationships. No more watching stolen cable, gambling, cheating on taxes, lying, or lusting. God is on top of things, making this world a better place. He is going to force us to be perfect. It was fine when God was stopping all those other dirty sinners, but as soon as He stops us in our tracks it doesn't feel so good. God complies with our choices; even those of a jaded lover, pedophile, or a bloodthirsty war general; even the choices that would place His son on a cross. It's not His perfect will, but it is His permissive will.

Reasons

It's difficult to accept the concept of a caring, compassionate, considerate God when we believe He's the one sending all the bad things in our lives. "Don't all things happen for a reason? Doesn't God orchestrate everything?" you're asking. No. Some things just happen. It is the sinful planet we live on. You can trace most of our illnesses, hardships, financial woes, and break-ups to our own bad decisions. Don't put those on God. We cause our own automobile accidents. We cause most of our own drama.

In Luke 13:1-5, Jesus was questioned by some people about the reasons for two tragic events of His time. Pilate had slaughtered innocent worshipers in the temple, apparently for no reason, and a tower had accidentally fallen and crushed 18 people. "Why did these things happen? Were they worse sinners than us?" Christ emphatically refutes such a claim by asking a rhetorical question: "Do you actually think they were worst sinners than you because they died in such a way?"

We all want explanations for misfortunes in life. We believe bad things can't happen without a reason. So we tell people who are suffering, "Everything happens for a reason!" It is insensitive and unfair for us to say such things. Stop trying to give people's cancer a purpose, and instead, give them purpose to get through it. That is what made Job's friends seem like his enemies. Unlike Job's remarks, most of the things his friends said about God were true. Their error was in trying to find a reason for Job's suffering. Not everything we go through has a purpose, but we can be purposeful in everything we go through. Not everything has a reason, but there is a reason to get through everything.

Although God does permit, or *authorize,* every negative thing we face in life, He is not the *author* of those negative things. God does not prevent us from facing life—good or bad. It is true that "all things work for the good of those who love the Lord" (Romans 8:28, NIV), but that simply means that God has a way of turning Red Seas, walls of Jericho, Goliaths, fiery furnaces, lions' dens, and Lazarus-like deaths into opportunities of great blessing. Just because we find blessing, growth, and wisdom at the end of trials doesn't mean that all the mayhem came from Him. God actually prefers that we learn things the easy way. He says to choose his way because it is easy, and His load is light (Matthew 11:30). Unfortunately, we typically learn the hard way. Fortunately, though, some of us still learn. A few more battle scars, but we learn. Forty years in the wilderness, but we learn.

So let's stop trying to figure out why God allowed a bus full of children to crash, leaving all of them dead. The driver fell asleep at the wheel. It's tragic, it's sad, it's sin, but it is not God. It wasn't by His design that your sister died of Leukemia or that your husband left you for another woman. It was not His perfect plan that your neighbor's son died in a boating accident or that your daughter was born with cerebral palsy.

Please don't think I am being insensitive. I have gone through such heart-wrenching trials that sometimes I wished I could fall asleep and never wake up. I have learned, however, that heartache, disappointment, failure, and death are all a part of life. It doesn't matter if you are rich or poor, black or white, male or female, believer or non-believer, created or Creator; if you have stepped foot on this planet, you have gone, or will go, through something that will make you want to scream and give up. At this point in Earth's history, it's just a fact of life.

Since life is going to hurl its unpredictable curve balls at us, maybe it is better for us to stop asking all the "whys" and start asking the "hows."

Lord, *how* do I get through this storm in my life?

How can I find the good in my tragedy?

How can I help my sister or brother through their pain?

The *whys* have us playing the role of victims. The *hows* prepare us to be victors.

Thanks for Looking Out

Job finally gets it. He's not God. It's a good thing he's not because he didn't know the first thing about running a universe. It's almost as if God was willing to give him a shot at His throne, just as long as he could answer the divine questionnaire. These were easy questions, if you were God. Job was not, and he never would be. Neither will we. So why don't we leave the God stuff up to the One who *was, is, and always will be* God.

For all of those who feel that God's response to Job was an arrogant mess of machismo and He avoided all the big questions by asking a bunch of vague questions, read Job's final response:

> Then Job replied to the LORD: "I know that you can do all things; no plan of yours can be thwarted. You asked, '*Who is this that obscures my counsel without knowledge?*' Surely I spoke of things I did not understand, things too wonderful for me to know. You said, '*Listen now, and I will speak; I will question you, and you shall answer me.*' My ears had heard of you but now my eyes have seen you. Therefore I despise myself and repent in dust and ashes." (Job 42:1-6, NIV)

Did you catch that? Job says he can now *see* God. The big nerd put on a pair of glasses that changed his outlook on life, pain, and his Creator. God's response couldn't have been more timely or fitting for the occasion. We have problems? God reminds us He is God. We have storms in our life? He reminds us He is the Calmer. We suffer from depression? Jesus reminds us that He is Joy. He is life! I once heard a preacher say, "Stop telling God how big your giants are, and start telling your giants how big your God is." Sometimes God's response to our perplexities is, "Don't you know who *I* am?"

Job's real concerns and questions are the same as ours. "Lord, do you know what you're doing up there? Are you who you say you are? Do you know how to fly this plane?" God gave Job just a few of His divine chores, and that was enough for him.

If you're responsible for feeding the birds and keeping the constellations in place all at the same time, surely you can handle my concerns. If you see the deer when she feeds her fawn, I know you have an attentive eye on me. If the universe is not too big for you, then surely my problems aren't too big for you. I was just checking-in to make sure you were still watching me—to see if you still cared. Forgive me for not trusting you. I thought I knew you. But now I can say I truly do. Thanks for taking the time to listen. Things are finally starting to look a whole lot clearer.

Tear Jerker

God was not concerned about putting Job in his place. He wanted to make Job aware of *His* place. He needed Job to understand that He cares and is concerned with even the smallest details in our lives. God is intimately connected to life and all its inner workings.

After speaking with Martha, Jesus asks her to call Mary, Lazarus' other sister, so that He might also comfort her. When Mary is brought before Jesus, she falls at His feet and says the same thing Martha said earlier, "Lord, *if* you had only come sooner, my brother would still be alive." By this time, a crowd of mourners had gathered around Jesus and Lazarus' sisters. Everyone is crying now, including Jesus. "Jesus wept" (John 11:35, NIV). It is the shortest verse in the Bible. I think that was intentional. It draws attention to just how *connected* Jesus is to us. Even the God of the universe, who had the power to change the current circumstance in the blink of an eye, took time to be one with humanity and cry with those who were deeply saddened by death and suffering.

Jesus wept. Where is God when you are hurting? Right here with you. He doesn't exit the room when we begin to cry in our loneliness or bitterness. He grabs some Kleenex and sits at the edge of the bed. With tears streaming down His cheeks, He gently rubs our shoulder. God weeps. He cries. Our pain touches Him. Jesus is "deeply moved in spirit and troubled" by our heartache (John 11:33, NIV). He's angry at the hardships that sin causes. He hates it just as much, and maybe even more, than we do. He hates it so much it *kills* Him.

In order for Christ to rid the world of all its unfairness, He subjected Himself to it. Not even Jesus received special treatment on earth. The Son of God didn't get a free pass. Some of His prayers were not answered according to His will. At times it felt like His father wasn't listening and didn't care. Sometimes His father was painfully silent. He was tempted, tested, and tried in every way we can imagine. He was the prince of human and divine suffering. That is why He weeps. He so closely identifies with our pain and grief that it would be impossible for Him not to cry. (Mark 14:36, 15:34; Hebrews 4:15)

I know some of you are still angry with Him. You were raped, molested, physically and emotionally abused. You were divorced, injured, and fired. You lost your home, car, and mind. Jesus, just standing there with a handkerchief and sobbing, is no comfort for you. Maybe Job eventually backed down and was manipulated by God's intimidation, but not you. You still have something to say. You still have a finger to point. You want a word with Him face to face? You want to know *where* God is when it hurts?

There is a large crowd around Him, but I think you can make it through. You are so desperate to see Jesus. You begin to move in-between the crowd. There are those who seem more determined than you and deliberately try to keep you behind them, but you are determined too. You are suddenly pushed to the ground, yet are not deterred, nor discouraged. You begin to crawl, squeezing past their legs. Dirt is getting kicked into your eyes, but you remain on course. Your anger fuels you. You know you are getting closer. If you can only grab hold of His clothes, maybe then He will notice you; maybe He will be forced to pay attention to your complaints. Maybe you can finally get answers and direction. People are stepping on your hands; it doesn't slow you down. You are persistent. You are focused. You are almost there. In fact, you can actually see His clothing. You stretch your hand out in desperation as if this is your one and only chance of reaching Him. You clasp a hold of His robe, but something is terribly wrong. It has blood on it. As you tug, you realize it is no longer attached to its owner. You scramble closer to find yourself at His feet. Something is definitely wrong. His feet … they are nailed to a wooden beam. You look up to see a bloodied, mangled body, twisting and writhing in pain on a cross. Each breath is delayed and labored. Drops of blood from His thorn-pierced brow are landing on the back of your hand. Look at Him. There He goes again—being silent. Here is your opportunity. Your intense effort has paid off. Rise to your feet. Tell Him what you think. Tell Him how He has never been there for you. Maybe you will never be able to give the one who hurt you an earful, but give it to the One who stands in his place. With your intense rage, tell Him how He cheated you and left you all alone. He has a listening ear. He's not going anywhere anytime soon, so go for it..................

Nothing to say? Calvary has a way of leaving us speechless. Quite an answer to our pain isn't it? This is what it looks like when God becomes the situation. Where is God when we are hurting? You can find Him on a mount called Calvary.

p.s.............

Chapter 5
— Life on a Limb —

"I am the vine; you are the branches. If a man remains in me and I in him, he will bear much fruit; apart from me you can do nothing." John 15:5, NIV

Zacchaeus had it all. He was rich. He was at the top of his profession. As the chief tax collector in his city, he wielded great power. Anything a man could want was at his fingertips—money, power, and respect. As with the young rich man, Zacchaeus also wanted to see Jesus. What is it about these wealthy guys that makes them want to bump into the Carpenter from Nazareth? Why are they so desperate for an encounter with Christ? Did Jesus owe the government back taxes? Did Zacchaeus also have angry words for God?

Maybe it was none of those issues, but it is hard for me to imagine why such a wealthy, successful entrepreneur would have anything to do with a peasant preacher. I used to think Jesus was only for the poor and desperate people who had nothing more than a prayer. I thought He was only for the folks who were down on their luck, not for those who were already prosperous.

King Solomon, another rich guy in the Bible, gives us insight into the mind of Zach. Solomon was one of the wealthiest, wisest, and most famous guys ever to walk this planet. He appeared to have everything. Check out a few blurbs from an article on Solomon in *Forbes Magazine*:

Solomon received about 25 tons of gold a year. (1 Kings 10:14, CEV)

King Solomon was greater in riches and wisdom than all the other kings of the earth. The whole world sought audience with Solomon to hear the wisdom God had put in his heart. Year after year, everyone who came brought a gift—articles of silver and gold, robes, weapons and spices, and horses and mules. (1 Kings 10:23-25, CEV)

What a write-up! I was even more excited when I picked up his article in *GQ Magazine*. I knew this guy had the secrets to happiness, success, and fulfillment. The article began with "Meaningless! Meaningless. … Utterly meaningless! Everything is meaningless" (Ecclesiastes 1:2, NIV).

I felt this was a terrible way to start the article, but I gave him a few paragraphs to warm up. He continues:

I said to myself, "Have fun and enjoy yourself!" But this didn't make sense. Laughing and having fun is crazy. What good does it do? I wanted to find out what was best for us during the short time we have on this earth. So I decided to make myself happy with wine and find out what it means to be foolish, without really being foolish myself. I did some great things. I built houses and planted vineyards. I had flower gardens and orchards full of fruit trees. And I had pools where I could get water for the trees. I owned slaves, and their sons and daughters became my slaves. I had more sheep and goats than anyone who had ever lived in Jerusalem. Foreign rulers brought me silver, gold, and precious treasures. Men and women sang for me, and I had many wives who gave me great pleasure. I was the most famous person who had ever lived in Jerusalem, and I was very wise. I got whatever I wanted and did whatever made me happy. But most of all, I enjoyed my work. Then I thought about everything I had done, including the hard work, and it was simply chasing the wind. Nothing on earth is worth the trouble. (Ecclesiastes 2:1-11, CEV)

Whoever loves money never has enough; whoever loves wealth is never satisfied with his income. This too is meaningless. (Ecclesiastes 5:10, NIV)

This was a devastating article for my future aspirations. How could such a wise man crush all our hopes and dreams? Don't we gain our fulfillment by acquiring more in life? Can't we measure our worth by our accomplishments? Apparently not.

Most of us have learned to measure our worth in terms of money, career, family, and possessions. We choose many positive things, such as education and careers, in order to find acceptance and add value to our lives. Even upon being introduced to people, it doesn't take long before we pop the big question: "So, what do you do?" It is our not-so-subtle way of assessing them. If you are proud of what you do, this is the fun part of the conversation. This is where you get to stick out your chest and talk about how special you are. However, if you aren't, this is where things get uncomfortable.

Why do we think our worth is determined by our accomplishments? Life is more than what we *do*. Our worth can never be measured in terms of what we do, but rather who we *are*. Again, we are the image of God! God calculates our worth apart from our cheating, stealing, lying, murdering, addictive selves. He places His immeasurable value on us apart from our degrees, promotions, marriages, children, and investment funds. We can do a world of good or a world of evil, and it still would not add to, or displace, our worth in His eyes. This is what Zach needed to hear. This is what he must have been searching for. This is why he needed to see Jesus.

Putting Yourself Out There

Zach was in luck because that afternoon Jesus was passing through the city. As Jesus' itinerary became public knowledge, the streets were filled with curious onlookers. There were those in the crowd that wanted to be healed of incurable diseases. Some needed to hear an encouraging word. And I'm sure more than a few *haters* were sprinkled throughout—the usual crowd. Then there was Zacchaeus who just wanted to see Him.

Even though Zach seemed to have it all, he did have one tiny problem. He was on the *wee* side of things. Zacchaeus was a very short guy. This small detail was big for a man trying to see Jesus surrounded by thousands of taller people (I'll stop with all the cheesy puns). I'm not sure what exactly Zach, with all his shortcomings, expected from a simple look at Jesus; but whatever it was, it was important enough for him to act like his size and not his age (last one, promise). He had his limo driver rush him to the closest tree on Jesus' route so that he could re-live a favorite childhood pastime—tree climbing. How humiliating. All the power and respect Zach had spent decades to achieve was lost when the people saw him remove his double-breasted blazer and scuff his alligator-skinned sandals all the way up the tree.

It can be a little embarrassing to put yourself out there to see Jesus. You are the star of the football team. You are the CEO of a company. You are a promising student. You are the ladies' man. You are the trophy girlfriend. You need to openly express your desire for Jesus, but you're not sure you want everyone else to know about it. They might think you are weak. They might even think you are a freak. It takes humility to see God. I know it will feel awkward to put yourself out there on a limb, but aren't you tired of hanging through life by a limb? Zach was weary of it for sure. He was fed up with his short man's complex running and ruining his life. He did not want to try to prove anything to anyone anymore. It didn't matter what anyone was going to think. He just wanted to see Jesus. If it meant he had to climb to the top of a tree in order to see Him, he was willing to do it.

Vantage Point

"Wait a second … here He comes! I can see Him! I can see Him!" Did anyone have a better limb than Zach? He had the best seat in the city to see Christ. No one was in the tree to distract him. The crowd seemed smaller, quieter and Jesus appeared bigger, clearer. We all need this type of tree experience in our lives. Regular, strategic vantage points where we can hear God more distinctly, and see Him more clearly. A place where the TV can't be turned on and the iPod won't work. Where the only cell phone reception you receive is from heaven's wireless provider. Where we can leave the world behind, in a sense, and be at the perfect place to talk with God, and listen to His word. It will feel strange at first, but when all the stress and noise hushes in your mind, you will know you came to right place.

Make a determined effort to seal off time in your busy day to be at a vantage point with God. Your life will be better for it. God does not want to add more to your already full plate. He actually wants to give you a plate with all those neat little partitions. A plate that keeps dressing and juices from getting all mixed up with each other (I hate it when that happens). A plate that places boundaries so your life tastes sweeter and is a whole lot neater (Ooh … that rhymed).

House Call

The crowd comes to a halt and hush as Jesus stops underneath Zach's tree. Jesus looks up with a big smile at the IRS rep sharing a branch with a chipmunk. "Zacchaeus, is that you? Come down from there right now! Man, I must go to your house today" (Luke 19:5). If most of the crowd was unaware of the whereabouts of their little tax collector friend, they all knew after Jesus put his business in the street.

Shocked by Jesus' invitation, I'm sure Zach's response went a little something like this: "Jesus, don't you know who I am? I'm not a perfect man. My house is not in shape for you to come over. I have certain posters on the wall that you wouldn't be pleased with. My movie collection would surely make you frown. If you were to check the history on my computer of the websites I visit, you would blush. I have beer in the fridge and weed on the coffee table. Oh yeah, I think Karen, Maricela, and Lashanda are still over there from last night's party. I'm hanging by a limb, man. Are you sure you want to come over?"

Isn't it comforting to know that Jesus was privy to this information and still wanted to show up at Zach's house? As a teenager, I got scared when my mom asked, "If Jesus were to come today, would you want to be caught with that filth on the wall?" She was referring to my *Prince* posters. She had me sweating it out with the prospect of Jesus catching me off guard. If I were Zacchaeus, I would be intimidated at the thought of this Holy guy showing up at my house. But nothing was going to keep Zach from having a personal encounter with God. Not his past, his addictions, or his fears. He desired transformation. He needed Jesus to come over. "Lord, I accept. Please, come to my home."

Painkillers

Zach is a good example of why we should never believe the "hype" of sin. No longer will I fall for the perception that people who are doing their "own thing" are having more fun than those who are following God. Zach is living a pretty comfy life, so why does he want to jeopardize it by meeting with Jesus? He's probably going to ask him to give up something.

We are a product of bad programming and false advertising. We are told that if we could only gain fame, love, and money, we will be happy. That is untrue. There are many unhappy millionaires out there. Famous people long for privacy and normalcy in their lives. Many couples, once passionately in love, are wondering where the spark went. Life has to be more than these things.

If we were truly honest about some of our so-called *fun* times in life, it would be extremely difficult to suppress the memories of all the headaches and heartaches that accompanied our choices for entertainment. No one likes to talk about being ditched after what he or she was hoping was more than a one-night stand. Few are willing to tell you that after a night of drunken fun with friends, they puked their insides out and had one of the worst hangovers. I am not even going to talk about the DUI or the wrecked car. I won't even comment about the ruined relationships because of our lies and infidelity. Gambling away our mortgage payment at the local casino is still a sensitive subject. We will save the topics of our addiction to food and shopping for another time. History is littered with lives destroyed by gluttony and greed. Sin's "fun" is an illusion.

All we do is pop painkillers. That's right. Many of our relationships, music, drugs, and workaholic schedules are nothing more than glorified painkillers. Our vices merely distract us from the pain in our lives. They do nothing to heal or restore us back to wholeness. Zach was tired of drugging the pain in his life. His career and reckless living could no longer conceal his unhappiness. The pain was pointing him to the problem areas in his life. It was time for a house call from the Divine Doctor. We don't need any more painkillers to mask our misery. We need a sure cure for this disease. We need to see Jesus.

I know some of us are still fearful of the thought of Jesus just dropping into our lives. Most of us aren't willing to see Him until we get our stuff together. It's as if we are uncomfortable with the doctor discovering our illness. We wish we could get well before he visits so he would be impressed with our health. Silly, isn't it?

In a world that glorifies success, an admission of weakness disarms pride at the same time that it prepares us to receive grace. ... In the presence of the Great Physician, [our] most appropriate contribution may be [our] wounds. —Phillip Yancey

No More Pillowcases

Growing up, my mom believed in keeping a clean house. Unfortunately, though, she wasn't always able to turn the belief into action (I hope she never reads this). I remember one day a close relative dropped by our house unannounced. Before cell phones, there were doorbells to signal that someone was coming over. My mom did not panic. She was prepared for these situations and my brothers and I knew the drill. We ran through the house closing all the bedroom doors. We did our best impersonation of human vacuums, picking up any clutter off the floor. She even had us do the unthinkable! She made us put all the dirty dishes in a pillowcase and throw them into the coat closet. You might wonder how we would have time to do all this before opening the door. We were really, really good. By the time the door was open, the house looked presentable. Our guest walked through the house saying, "Girl, you sure do keep a clean house."

"You know me, girl," my mom would confidently reply. Of course my brothers and I were too busy gasping for air to say hello.

Is that what we're going to do when God shows up at our door? When we look through the peephole and see Him standing outside, we'll run to rip down the posters? We'll toss out the questionable CDs and DVDs? We'll trash some items on our desktop? I'm ready Jesus! Are we? Or are we just giving the mere appearance of a person who has his or her home and heart in order? We can't fool God. We look ridiculous when we try to hide our stuff from Him. He sees everything. He knows you—even down to the very number of hairs on your head (Matthew 10:30).

So no more pretending. No more believing in sin's hype. No more pillowcases. Don't wait until you no longer feel guilty. Don't let your shortcomings get in the way any longer. When Christ knocks on the door, do not be scared. Be relieved. He has come to help. Let Him in while the pain and mistakes are still fresh and people are waiting around holding rocks to throw at you. A last minute clean up could never prepare you for Jesus' arrival. He knows you too well. He knows what's in the closet. He knows what is stored on your computer. He knows what is under the bed. He knows what is beneath the surface, so stop trying to hide your stuff. Just be like Zach. *Lord, my house and heart are a mess; please come over.* Put yourself out there on a limb so Christ can clearly see you, and you can clearly see Him.

p.s. Two thousand years ago Jesus was so desperate for you to see Him that He humbled Himself and was taken up on a tree.

Chapter 6

— Too Good to Pass Up —

*"If you obey my commands, you will remain in my love,
just as I have obeyed my Father's commands and remain
in his love. I have told you this so that my joy may be in
you and that your joy may be complete. ... This is my
command: Love each other." John 15:10-11, 17, NIV*

The first car I bought with my own money was affectionately named "The Bucket." It was a big, blue, boat-looking Buick on balding tires. I paid a whopping one hundred dollars for it. The car was a steal at that price. The owner needed fast cash and I couldn't miss an opportunity to help someone. There was one big catch with this car, though—it didn't have any brakes. Well, it kind of did, but not really. In order for the car to come to a legal stop you had to be driving about fifteen miles per hour. If you were driving any faster and applied the brakes, the car would spinout and come to a stop in the lane of oncoming traffic. How did I know that? Well, let's just say that I had a few experiences with this car.

Not having brakes wasn't supposed to be that big of a deal because I was only going to drive around my college campus. However, safety was thrown out the window when my girlfriend successfully begged me to drive her to the mall—a destination that happened to be over an hour away. The things we do for love. I prayed for all the traffic lights to be green the whole way there. You can imagine how frustrated people were with me when I had to slow down to a crawl just to exit the freeway. How I made it to the mall and back was nothing short of a miracle. Just because I went to college doesn't mean I was smart.

At times, we foolishly feel we are impervious to the consequences of our poor choices in life. We all feel that way until we find our lives spun-out in the wrong lane, facing a huge semi-truck with its blinding head beams careening dangerously towards us. Just in case you missed the license number of that truck, it's D-R-A-M-A.

Something has to give. Somewhere along the way we must come to our senses and realize there is a better way of doing things. A way that is healthier. A way that is happier.

Rolling Stones

By this time, a crowd had assembled around the tomb of Lazarus which had a large stone in front of the entrance. Jesus turned to some of the men who were standing by and said, "Roll the stone away." Now Christ could have easily used *the force* like a Jedi, and moved the stone Himself. However, the people standing around could have moved the stone as well. They would have to get their hands dirty, but they could do it.

We have a part to play in improving our lives, and the lives of people around us. God wants our cooperation in changing our negative circumstances. He is not going to do for us what we can do for ourselves. You want to marry the person of your dreams, but have you done all you can to be "dreamy" yourself? You want the new job, but have you made it, through hard work and responsibility, impossible for them not to give you the opportunity? God will do His part, but are you willing to do yours? *Roll the stone away.*

Rolling stones away is not just about us. It's also, more importantly, about helping others. Understand that Lazarus could not roll his own stone away. He was a bit indisposed. You want to live in a better world, but what are you doing to make it happen? We must accept that we have a responsibility in making this world a better place. We have to do our part. We need to get involved in fighting injustices and reaching out to the impoverished. People think God doesn't care because they see we don't care. We need to flood this planet with acts of kindness, compassion, and love. I know that sounds cute, flowery, cheesy, and a little like the names of a few Care Bears, but if everyone embraced this mission, the earth would be a bit more like heaven.

So, no more blaming God for all the problems in the world. Stop asking "how could He allow people to go hungry?" God is entrusting us to put an end to world hunger. No more drive-bys of people in need, praying, "Oh, Lord, please bless that person," because all God is going to say is, "Great! I thought you'd never ask. Now pull over. I'm going to feed them through you." Again, God will not do anything that we are more than capable of doing ourselves. Our *participation* is required. Get your hands dirty, and *roll the stone away.*

Give Until It Feels Good

Jesus' visit to Zacchaeus' home and heart led him to stand up at the dinner table and make the most unlikely statement. "Look, Lord! Here and now I give half of my possessions to the poor, and if I have cheated anybody out of anything, I will pay back four times the amount" (Luke 19:8, NIV). Did you catch that? Zach is giving up the timeshare in Rome, the Galilean yacht, the getaway chateau in the plush Canaan Hills, even the four-horse powered, gold-plated chariot with the 42-inch silver rims. Zach is now willing to live as a mere peasant after his meeting with Jesus. Christ did not have to give the same speech he gave the young rich guy about selling everything he had and helping the poor. Zach had failed to find happiness in wealth alone. Therefore, why should he have held on to it any longer when there were others whose needs were so much greater than his own?

When Zack gave his money purpose, it revived him to a level of joy he never knew existed. It feels good to give. Like it or not, we are wired to get a high from helping people. It is the part of our original DNA that sin has not completely erased from our gene pool. It's the breath of God in us that still responds to its natural habitat of being a giver like our Creator. Books and television shows are now encouraging people to get behind the phenomenal concept of giving. It's contagious. The world is catching on to the old adage "It is better to give than to receive" (Acts 20:35). Now I wonder who said that? Oh yes, it was Jesus.

Most of you already know this to be true. You know how much work it can take to give of yourself to the community, church, and family. But doesn't it feel great knowing that you spent quality time making someone else's life worth living? This is the best part of being like God. The "get more" game should never be played because we always end up losing in the end. We waste a whole lot of time, energy, and money in the process. I like the "give more" game better.

Does it mean that toys, relationships, money, and careers are bad and should be avoided? Of course not. It's only bad when we attempt to use those things to replace something that is irreplaceable. Jesus says, "Seek first the kingdom of God and his righteousness, and all these things will be given to you as well" (Matthew 6:33, NIV). God blessed thousands of people through Zacchaeus' generosity, and He is eager to do the same through you. *Roll the stone away.*

I Have a Feeling About This

I know that doing some of the things God tells us to do doesn't always initially feel good. However, I have learned not everything that feels good *is* good. Like so many, I used to think my feelings were sent from God. If I felt drawn to someone with intensity, I thought, "Surely God is behind this. If not, why would he allow me to feel this way?" I eventually learned that our feelings are just that—*our* feelings. Our feelings can't be trusted because we are too fickle. Hot one moment, cold the next—on and off. It's just a part of being human. That is why I have learned to be thankful for God's involvement in my life. He keeps me focused, especially when my feelings cannot be trusted. God guarantees our happiness when we are following Him. "Those who hear the Word of God and obey it *are happy*" (Luke 11:28, NLV). Anthony De Mello writes in his book, *The Way to Love*:

> *Recall the kind of feeling you have when you succeed, when you have made it, when you get to the top, when you win a game or a bet or an argument. And contrast it with the kind of feeling you get when you really enjoy the job you are doing … notice the qualitative difference between the worldly feeling and the soul feeling. … Remember what you felt like when you had power, you were the boss, people looked up to you, took orders from you; or when you were popular. And contrast that worldly feeling with the feeling of intimacy, companionship—the times you thoroughly enjoyed yourself in the company of a friend or with a group in which there was fun and laughter.*
>
> *Having done this, attempt to understand the true nature of worldly feelings, namely, the feelings of self-promotion, self-glorification. They are not natural; they were invented by your society and your culture. … These feelings do not produce the nourishment and happiness that is produced when one contemplates Nature or enjoys the company of one's friends or one's work. They were meant to produce thrills, excitement—and emptiness.*

Zach was tired of feeling empty. Jesus was offering something better and he wanted in on it. Zach offered to give up everything without a struggle because it became a privilege to follow Jesus. Worldly things had finally lost their excitement. The opportunity to do good was simply too good to pass up. The possibility of being better and giving life his best actually seemed possible.

Happiness to Perfection

Why does God want us to give our very best in life? The better question is "why not?" Zacchaeus voluntarily gave up everything to follow Jesus simply because the opportunity was there for the taking. Jesus says, "Be perfect as your heavenly father is perfect" (Matthew 5:48, NIV). We want the perfect husband, the perfect girlfriend, the perfect job, and the perfect house. Why should we strive for anything less when it comes to matters of character and lifestyle? Don't you hope your favorite team completes a perfect season? Even if it is highly unlikely, every team begins the season with the goal to win every game. The game is more fun to play and watch when our team gives it their best. Life is the same way. When we give it our best, life is simply better. Jesus wants us to live life abundantly (John 10:10). Christ's invitation to follow Him is an opportunity to a happier, more fulfilling life.

When Jesus told the adulteress that He didn't accuse or condemn her, He followed that statement with, "You may go now, *but don't sin anymore*" (John 8:11, CEV). It was great news to hear Christ say He did not accuse her. However, the reality of letting her baggage go and the challenge of living a healthier, more fulfilling life was even better. The woman, like Zach, felt empty and confused about her direction in life. Jesus was offering her an alternative. She had been convinced she would never amount to anything; certain her circumstances would never change. Then Christ came along and not only is she forgiven, but she can now respect herself and set a new course in life. "Don't sin anymore" was just the breakthrough she was looking for.

Living a life of sin is just too burdensome. That is why Jesus is so insistent on you following Him. His way is easier and His burden is lighter (Matthew 11:30). God's way should make life easier—He is the Creator, isn't He? The Creator of all things should have an idea of what works and doesn't work. He should know what makes us tick. C.S. Lewis writes in the ever-popular book, *Mere Christianity*:

God made us: invented us as a man invents an engine. A car is made to run on petrol, and it would not run properly on anything else. Now God designed the human machine to run on himself. He Himself is the fuel our spirits were designed to burn, or the food our spirits were designed to feed on. There is no other. That is why it is just no good asking God to make us happy in our own way. ... God cannot give us a happiness and peace apart from Himself, because it is not there. There is no such thing ... the machine conks. It seems to start up all right and runs a few yards, and then it breaks down. They are trying to run it on the wrong juice.

Can you imagine your car begging you to put Kool-Aid in the gas tank? Can you see your grandparents trying to shove a VHS tape into a DVD player? We laugh at these scenarios, but we look equally senseless trying to find happiness and joy outside of God's plan for our lives. Just like the car was designed to run on gasoline, we were designed to live by His principles. Again, it's in our DNA. It's our original factory settings. I know we are all born into sin and those settings have been altered. However, our mind, body, and soul respond more healthily to God's original design and purpose for our lives. We cannot have true happiness apart from God. It simply does not exist. There is no such thing. Any attempt to find happiness and satisfaction apart from Him is a journey into a world of make-believe.

Christ desires to resurrect and revive you into a new way of living. You do not have to live entombed any longer. Christ's invitation for us to follow Him is truly an opportunity for a better life. Please, do not think if you choose to follow Jesus you have just revoked your license to have fun and enjoy life. This is not an invitation to a boring lifestyle. The Creator knows a thing or two about happiness since He happens to be the inventor of it.

I'm glad I've been asked to follow God. I'm inspired to cooperate with Him by rolling stones away. I consider it an honor and a privilege to be like God. He loves and accepts us just the way we are. Yet, He loves us so much that He doesn't want us to *remain* just the way we are. He will come to our home, dirty pillowcases and all. However, God does not want to leave our homes and hearts the way He found them. So let's start focusing on the privileged opportunity of following the One we were created to be like. I *have to* be perfect? No! I *get to* be perfect? Yes!!!!! With Christ in the picture it is possible. With God *all* things are possible.

p.s. "Everything you were taught can be put into a few words: Respect and obey God! This is what life is all about."—King Solomon (Ecclesiastes 12:13, CEV)

Chapter 7

── To the Highest Bidder ──

"Greater love has no one than this, that he lay down his life for his friends." John 15:13, NIV

I t was about eight years ago when I was introduced to the wonderful world of eBay. I was sharing with my buddy, Daniel, about my childhood pleasures and all the toys I had, or wished I had, growing up. He then told me that I could find some of those same toys on an online auction site called eBay. People from all over the world would simply sell their valuables, or garbage, on eBay where truly "one person's trash is another person's treasure." I went online and typed in the name of the first toy I wanted to see. O-P-T-I-M-U-S_P-R-I-M-E, enter. Wow! Over three hundred listings displayed. I clicked on one of the auctions and there was a little picture of the Transformers toy I used to have. I started singing the song, "Transformers, more than meets the eye. … " I was so excited. Daniel told me that all I had to do was place how much money I was willing to bid and wait to see if I win the auction. I figured that wouldn't be a problem given the fact that the toy was almost 20-years-old and a little beat-up. It would probably be only a few dollars. Wishful thinking. It seems I wasn't the only person trying to recapture his childhood. My precious Optimus Prime was going for over two hundred dollars!

There were still a few days left for the auction, but there was no way I was going to pay two hundred dollars for a toy that only cost me ten dollars 20 years ago. But as I looked at the picture, I grew more and more enamored with the thought of bringing the little guy home. I want to tell you that I ignored my nostalgic impulses to pay such an exorbitant amount—that I stood up for sound, financial sensibility. However, I began what could only be called an obsession for reclaiming, or *redeeming*, many of my little, lost, plastic babies. It took me several years and thousands of dollars before I kicked my eBay habit.

Redemption

Redemption is one of those big words in the Bible we often hear. In fact, our Christian faith hinges on the theme of God redeeming His people. According to Merriam-Webster's dictionary, the word "redeem" means to buy back, win back, or free from captivity by payment of ransom. The Bible tells us that Christ came to redeem us and offered His life as a ransom. "Even as the Son of man came not to be ministered unto, but to minister, and to give his life a ransom for many. ... Who gave himself a ransom for all. ... " (Matthew 20:28, 1 Timothy 2:6, NIV).

Christ giving His life as a ransom is the most widely accepted belief among Christians, regardless of denomination. Most of us are familiar with the concept of a ransom, where a price is set to secure one's freedom. The part that was always confusing to me, though, was to whom did Jesus have to pay the ransom? He is not redeeming us from the hands of an angry God because Paul tells us He is reconciling us back to the Father. "God was reconciling the world to himself in Christ, not counting men's sins against them" (2 Cor. 5:19, NIV). In other words, Jesus did not have to pay the Father to get us back. So, from whom, or what, is He redeeming us?

The Price is Right

When Satan tempted Jesus in the wilderness, he offered to give Him the kingdoms of this world if Christ only worshiped him. That struck me. Did Satan really have the kind of authority to make such an offer? Jesus often referred to Satan as the "prince" or "ruler" of this world (John 12:31, 14:30, 16:11). The apostle Paul refers to him as the "god" of this world (2 Cor. 4:4). Remember in the board meeting of Job's story how Satan represented Earth? It appears as if Satan has his name on the deed of this planet.

When God created Adam and Eve, He gave them dominion over the world. They were to be the rulers of this earth. When they decided to follow the old serpent and believe his lies, they pledged their allegiance to him. They essentially handed over their rights to their property. That is why Paul writes that death reigned over the earth after Adam's sin (Romans 5:12). The world was now under the curse of the enemy, sin, and death. This explains why so many Bible stories are bloody and filled with death. There are only two chapters in the entire Bible, Genesis one and two, where this curse does not exist and is not mentioned. We only see a perfect world in two chapters! The rest is God doing His best to work His ideals within Satan's government. Jesus wanted to redeem us from this administration of sin and death and all its consequences. No price was too high.

Power Struggle

Why would God give so much power over to Satan? I'll answer that with another question. Why did God give so much power and authority to Pilate during Jesus' trial? "Don't you realize I have power either to free you or to crucify you?" Pilate threatened. Jesus answered, "You would have no power over me if it were not given to you from above" (John 19:10-11, NIV). God has no problem laying aside His power or giving authority to others, because for Him the issue has never been about who is more powerful. God refuses to take anything back (redeem) by force. He wasn't going to flex His muscles and snatch us out of Satan's grip. It wouldn't prove anything more than the fact that He's stronger, and everyone already knew that, including Satan.

Author Ellen White wrote in her book, *The Desire of Ages*:

> *God could have destroyed Satan and his sympathizers as easily as one can cast a pebble to the earth; but He did not do this. Rebellion was not to be overcome by force. Compelling power is found only under Satan's government. The Lord's principles are not of this order. His authority rests upon goodness, mercy, and love; and the presentation of these principles is the means to be used. God's government is moral, and truth and love are to be the prevailing power.*

Remember, for God this is not a power struggle. This is a character contest. We already know who is more powerful. Your trust is what is up for grabs. Who do you trust? Who will get your vote?

Playing Devil's Advocate

Satan won a small planet called Earth. God wanted it back, but He wasn't going to punch Satan in the nose to get it. Satan knew this because he knows God. He didn't care about the two humans he tricked into disobeying God. They were just his bait. He had a bigger fish to fry.

Satan wanted to bring down the One who kicked him and his angel buddies out of heaven. They only wanted to shake things up a little and do their own thing, but God knew how poisonous sin was. Satan's ideologies could not co-exist in heaven with God's perfect principles, so he and his followers had to go. Satan figured since he was able to convince one-third of heaven's angels to follow him, surely he could convince the whole universe with a little more time and leverage. The humans were his leverage. *"If you want them, Creator, come and get them."*

Satan wanted to lure God into finishing the war that began in heaven, here on earth. He wanted to prove once and for all that God's principles were unnecessary and pointless for beings that could decide for themselves what was right or wrong. He wanted to prove that just because God is the Creator, doesn't mean he should make all the rules. All Satan wanted was for God to come down to his playground so that he could show Him to be a fraud. Forget testing Job, he wanted to test the Creator of the universe. There was only one catch. God had to come without His superpowers. He would have to fight this battle as a mortal. Character, and character alone, would be the deciding factor. If you were Satan, wouldn't you gladly welcome the opportunity for God to come down to your turf? Jesus, God the Son, step into the ring (John 1:1-4, 14).

God was determined to come to this earth in order to buy us back, but it was going to cost more than a few hundred dollars. It was going to cost Him much more dearly. It was going to cost Him His life. Satan wanted another shot at taking God down, and His blood was the ransom price. "For you knew that it was not with perishable things such as silver or gold that you were redeemed from the empty way of life handed down to you from your forefathers, but with the precious blood of Christ, a lamb without blemish or defect" (1 Peter 1:18-19, NIV).

God's Advocate

God would do anything to rid the universe of sin, forever, but He wasn't going to be a bully about it. God wanted to redeem us, but He knew if we were ever going to trust Him, we needed to get to know Him (Jeremiah 9:23-24). So, He came to earth. If after getting to know Him we wanted to come back to Him, the path home would be paved with His blood, sweat, and tears.

"Where are you? Why are you hiding?" God asked Adam and Eve in the garden. He has been asking that question ever since. Sin makes God look scary and angry to us. We run from Him instead of to Him.

The sound of God's footsteps in the garden used to bring such thrill of anticipation, but the knowledge and familiarity with evil had distorted that sound and made it dreadful. Why was it necessary for Jesus to come to earth? Because we kept running and hiding. The only way He could draw us out of hiding was if He became one of us. God is not too scary in diapers, learning how to walk, or with His first pimple.

God decided to become one of us. *Emmanuel,* "God with us" (Matthew 1:23, KJV). He had tried to invite us out of hiding through His friendship with Abraham, but was unsuccessful. He attempted to draw us out through His faithfulness to Joseph, but it was also ineffective. He even tried with His laws, given through Moses, but that just made Him more intimidating. From King David who had a heart like God's, to Daniel whose prophecies and prayers convinced a nation to hope again, men and women continued to run and hide from their Creator.

God's friends were never perfect "reps." If you need a job done right, then you better do it yourself. It was time for a new agreement to be drawn up (Jeremiah 31:31-33). There was nothing wrong with the old one except that we didn't keep it. We kept breaking the laws. So God would have to come to us personally. He would live out the old covenant flawlessly. He would show us His love, kindness, compassion, and patience in such a real, practical, and intimate way that there would be no mistaking what God is like. God would no longer be scary. God would be approachable. Children would want to play around Him. God would finally draw us out of hiding.

The author of the book of Hebrews writes:

In the past God spoke to our ancestors through the prophets many times and in many different ways. But now in these last days God has spoken to us through his Son. God has chosen his Son to own all things, and through him he made the world. The Son reflects the glory of God and shows exactly what God is like. (Hebrews 1:1-3, NIV)

Jesus proclaims to the Father, "I have brought you glory on earth by completing the work you gave me to do" (John 17:4, NIV). Jesus claims to have *completed* His work before His death! Why? Because the assignment that the Father gave His Son was to reveal the glory of God—to reveal God's person and character. I used to think that Jesus' only purpose in coming to this earth was to die, but now it sounds like His purpose was to live. He came to tell us the truth about God. Jesus tells Pilate during His trial, "For this reason I was born, and for this I came into the world, to testify to the truth" (John 18:37, NIV). Jesus was so convinced of the importance of the truth and knowledge of God's character that He equated it to eternal life. "Now this is eternal life: that they may *know you*, the only true God, and Jesus Christ, whom you have sent" (John 17:3, NIV). God came in order to be known. He was convinced that you would choose Him and His will if you only knew the truth—if you only knew Him.

It would have been easier had Christ just accepted Satan's offer in the wilderness to worship him in exchange for the world. How simple Christ's mission could have been with a quick phone call upstairs to inform His Father He had found an easier way to win back the kids. No long, drawn out litigations. Just a quick handshake, and the transfer would be complete. What Satan didn't realize, however, is that Jesus was not about the mere repossession of mankind, but about their transformation. What good would it have been for Jesus to deliver an unrepentant, unchanged, and unfit people to heaven's doorstep just to see history repeat itself? People needed to know God. This could only happen by Jesus living among the people. This could only happen by the people being able to see and feel God.

The bidding war had begun. Would God's character and principles prevail, or would He be exposed as a lying tyrant? God could lose all credibility if Jesus was unable to live up to His own principles. Satan was going to see to it that Christ failed. He would throw everything at Him, including a cross.

I know there are some of you who feel God could never be held captive, or be a part of anyone's negotiations. *"God can do anything He wants!"* That was the same problem everyone had when they saw the Son of God, after intense negotiations, held captive, and forced to carry His cross to His death. *"He surely could not be the Christ!"*

Remember, this is not about what God *can* do, because He can do anything He well pleases. It's about what God *chose* to do. He chose the path of *most* resistance. He chose the path that will rid sin from the universe forever. Again, God will not coerce us to serve Him, befriend Him, or return to Him by any manipulative means. He just wants to be Himself, and hopefully, that will be enough.

p.s. God could have left us to die, but He saw a picture of our world and said, "I'll do anything to get them back." Of course, we were going to cost Him much more than He paid for us in the beginning, but He willingly placed His bid. Yeah, we are old and beat-up, but He would do anything to get us back.

Chapter 8

—— The Good, the Bad, and the Ugly ——

"If I had not come and spoken to them, they
would not be guilty of sin. Now, however, they
have no excuse for their sin." John 15:22, NIV

As a child, there was one thing that would frighten me—the cross. Most kids were scared of the *Nightmare on Elm Street* and *Friday the 13*th movies. Not me. *Jesus of Nazareth, King of Kings, The Greatest Story Ever Told*, and any other movie depicting Christ's suffering and death would keep me up at night. My mother told me of a reaction I had when I was four-years-old to a movie dramatizing the suffering of Christ. She said I walked up to the TV screen and began hitting it screaming, "Don't do that to my Jesus!" It was traumatizing for me. I couldn't even be alone in a room if there were a painting hanging on the wall depicting Jesus' crucifixion. The picture of a dying Savior was haunting.

My fear was based on a sense of confusion on the matter. I just didn't understand it. I didn't understand how someone so good had to suffer so much. I became angry with God because He allowed such an injustice to happen. To hear from teachers and pastors that it was all part of His plan only made matters worse. How could God be behind that? I hated the cross. I hated the word *crucifixion*. Today, I still do.

Questions

One of the problems I had with the cross is that I didn't understand its purpose. When people tried to explain it to me, it didn't make sense. So maybe Jesus had to give His life as a ransom for us, but why did He have to die on a cross? Why not just jump headfirst off the top of the temple like Satan suggested in the wilderness? Why not ask that back-stabber, Judas, to literally stab him in the back with a knife? The Jews could have stoned Him. There were a hundred ways Christ could have laid down His life. Why the cross? I heard many interpretations, but none seemed to fit the logic of my young mind. Like many people during Paul's day, the cross was my "stumbling block" (1 Corinthians 1:23, NIV).

Another issue I had with the cross is that it had too many variables that just didn't line up with God's character. Did God invent the cross or did the Romans? Did He need Judas to betray Jesus, or Pilate to condemn Him? Did God's people really have a choice in rejecting Christ if He *had to* die on the cross? See, it's problematic. All these scenarios required people to do evil in order to accomplish God's will and that would mean some sin is necessary. I don't think God the Father, Son, and Spirit sat down around a table and said, "Yeah, we'll just have one of us nailed to a tree and call it a day. Who wants to be the One born in a manger?" The cross could not have been God's invention.

Lastly, if God is God and presumably makes up all the rules, then why can't He just forgive Adam and Eve for their mistake and move on? Why does it have to get all bloody? I don't cut off my hand in order to forgive someone who has offended me, so why does He have to nail His? I wasn't sure I wanted to be friends with someone who had to be tortured in order to be my friend. God, if you can do all things, find another way of forgiving sinful man and saving us from self-destruction.

Who Killed Christ?

Let's just clear up one thing. No one can kill God. He is life. Jesus says, "The reason my Father loves me is that *I lay down my life*—only to take it up again. No one takes it from me, but I lay it down of my own accord. I have authority to lay it down and authority to take it up again" (John 10:17-18, NIV). The Romans and Jews weren't responsible for killing Jesus because they never possessed such powers. Jesus was the one who gave up His spirit at the appointed time (John 19:30). What the Jews and Romans were responsible for was the scourging, the bruises, the spitting, and the nailing, but the *death* part Jesus did all by Himself. Death came only when Christ gave up His spirit (Matthew 27:50). Even Pilate was surprised when he heard that Jesus was dead after only six hours on the cross (Mark 15:44).

In the sacrificial ceremonies given to the Jews by God, Christ is represented by the High Priest, as well as the sacrificial lamb (Hebrews 9:11-12). He raised the knife, and He was the one the knife pierced. He is both the slayer of the lamb, and the "lamb that was slain" (Rev. 4:12, KJV). In that picture, there is no room for human cooperation. In other words, Judas and Pilate were unnecessary figures. The only reason they were in the picture was because they chose to be.

Christ told His disciples in the Garden of Gethsemane, the night before His death, "My soul is overwhelmed with sorrow to the point of death" (Matthew 26:38, NIV). The gospel writer, Luke, wrote that Jesus' sweat was "like drops of blood" while He was praying to His Father for another way out (Luke 22:44, NIV). Jesus was shedding blood before anyone laid a finger on Him. Why? Because His suffering was divine. He was experiencing the beginning of God's wrath. What is God's wrath? It is the worse thing He could ever do—turn away. The Father was withdrawing from His Son, and it was unbearable. "Daddy, daddy, why have you left me?" (Matthew 27:46).

God separating from His creation is ultimate result of sin. This is what Jesus was experiencing. This was the cost for our freedom. I'm convinced that if an angel from heaven had not been sent to comfort and encourage Jesus during this time of extreme anguish, He would have never made it out of that garden alive. Christ could have paid the price for redemption in a rocking chair. It seems, however, that would not be good enough for some. They wanted it to be gory.

A Public Spectacle

So if Christ giving up His life was a God thing, why did the Jews, Romans, and Satan play a role in these final scenes? Frankly, they wanted to be a part of all the drama. The majority of Jewish religious leaders wanted it to be a public spectacle. They wanted everyone to see that Jesus couldn't possibly be the Christ (Anointed One, Messiah), because their vision of the Christ—a super-powered combo of Samson's strength, David's courage, and Elisha's miracles—would never allow himself to undergo such abuse and humiliation. These religious leaders also wanted it to be a Roman-sanctioned execution so that no one could accuse them of the death of Jesus, which would have incited the crowd to hate them for killing someone who was, at the very least, a prophet of God. Jesus' enemies could have taken Him at any time (and they tried), but they were always afraid of the people who loved Him (which were too many to count). This is why the Jewish sanctioned trial for Jesus was in the early hours of the morning while everyone was asleep. Had the proceedings taken place in the open, the majority of the Jewish nation would never have allowed their leaders to arrest their "hero".

For the Romans it was simple. They just wanted it to be a publicly held, humiliating spectacle to make an example of anyone trying to assert himself as a king who could rival their Caesar. This is what the Romans did to those who professed to be the Jews' Messiah. This was also one of the reasons Jesus was so quiet about being the Christ until the appointed time (Matthew 16:20, John 12:20-36). It did not take a rocket scientist to figure out that you were asking for a death sentence if you made such bold assertions about yourself during this occupation of Roman rule. Jesus was well aware of what happened to those would-be Christs who came before Him. They were made examples of by being nailed to crosses. He knew when to profess to all of His friends and enemies, Roman and Jewish, *"I am He"* (John 18:5, NIV; Matthew 16:20, 26:64, 27:11; John 4:25-26, 18:37).

Satan wanted it to be a public execution to arouse the wrath of the Son of God. If he could have provoked Jesus to curse the soldiers, instead of forgiving them, he would have succeeded. If He could have convinced Him to call fire down from heaven to consume His tormentors, Satan would have won. Satan tested and tempted every fiber of Jesus' divinity and humanity hoping that when Christ realized everyone had abandoned Him, including His Father, He would be compelled to give up.

See You at the Movies

I know some of you are screaming, "What about prophecy?! Didn't all of this have to happen the way it was foretold?" Many of us view the prophecies of Christ's death as God preparing a script for us, saying, "Here, read your part." However, that particular prophecy is more like the script *we* wrote and told God, "Here, read your part." According to Jesus, God was not in control of these scenes, but rather "darkness [was] in control" (Luke 22:53, CEV).

Imagine watching your favorite movie on DVD. You watch this movie knowing full well that you had nothing to do with writing the script, directing the actors, or planning the special effects. The outcome of the movie has already been decided, but not by you. Just because God has the divine ability to pop in the DVD of *The Passion of the Christ* and see it before it opened in theaters, doesn't mean He wrote the script. We wrote it, and Christ decided to read for our part. Remember, God switched actors. The part that Adam, you, and I should have read for, which would have led us to Calvary, was now His responsibility.

I can understand God just wanting to walk out during the movie because it was so horrible. Even knowing what a terrible picture it was going to be, He remained in His seat. He wanted to remain with us during the good, the bad, and the ugly. The Father sat in silence, holding His breath at the closing scene as the Son, fastened to His seat, gave up His breath.

Boast in the Cross?

The symbol of the cross is intimately identified with Christianity for obvious reasons. It is the Christian mascot for salvation. The apostle Paul encouraged that positive link by often boasting about the cross of Christ in his letters (Galatians 6:14). However, it is interesting to note that two of Jesus' closest disciples, Peter and John, didn't really touch the subject of the cross in their writings. Read their letters in the Bible. Among the two, only once does Peter refer to the cross by name. Why? They were there. There was nothing wonderful about that day. The first century Christians would never have dared to use the symbol of the cross to identify their allegiance to Christ. The early church used the symbol of the fish (Ichthys), which we see on the back of cars today. Why didn't they use a cross as a symbol of Christianity? Because some of them were still being tortured and put to death on crosses. The cross represents the worst of man and sin. It represents man's intense hatred for God. I know Hollywood and our Easter pageants have us talking about good acting and special effects, but sometimes I think we are too desensitized to Calvary. The mere sight of the cross should cause us to say, "My God, my God, what have I done?"

The cross shows us how dark people's minds are and how deceptive sin is. Sin is so masterfully disguised that we don't notice it until it has bitten us and injected its deadly venom into our veins. It is similar to when the children of Israel were traveling through the wilderness on their way to the Promised Land. They kept pushing God away through their stubbornness and disobedience. Finally, God respected their wishes and backed off. When He did, poisonous snakes began biting the Israelites. They prayed to God and begged for His mercy to heal them from the deadly poison. God instructed Moses to mold a snake out of bronze, place it on a pole, and have the people to look at it in order to be healed (Numbers 21:4-9). It was as if God wanted them to take a good look at what rebellion and sin looks like. Just maybe that awful picture of the poisonous bronze snake would make them remember the consequences of their choices. God is hoping that Christ on the cross has that same effect on you. Sin is ugly and we shouldn't want any part of it after witnessing Calvary.

Why the Cross?

I understand why Christ's enemies chose the cross for Him. But why was Jesus so willing to accept their choice? Up until the cross, the universe kind of sympathized with God's former left-hand man, Lucifer. Maybe God had been a little harsh, kicking Satan out of heaven. A little sin really never hurt anybody, right? Calvary changed that perception. The cross demonstrated all the gross injustices in this world. Everyone saw Satan for who he really was. Sin was exposed, not as a wonderful alternative to God's plan, but as a gross, sadistic path that leads to death and destruction. Sin only brings ruin and regret.

Instead of exposing God, Satan exposed himself at the cross. Through Jesus' life we see the perfect character of God. Through His death, we see the wicked character of His enemy, and it was on display for the whole universe to see. This redemption thing was much bigger than our planet Earth. Paul writes, "And God was pleased for [Jesus] to make peace by sacrificing his blood on the cross, so that all beings in *heaven and on earth* would be brought back to God" (Colossians 1:20, CEV).

After Calvary, Satan wasn't allowed to show up for anymore of those heavenly board meetings. After witnessing the works of his hands, angels couldn't even hold their breakfast when they looked at him. Satan had no more sympathizers. He had revealed himself as a liar and a fraud. The cross was the low point in history. Yet, even when Satan was at his worst, God was at His very best. The Creator's principles for life and happiness held up even under the most excruciating circumstances. There could be no denying it. At Calvary, God was truly seen as good, and Satan and sin were clearly seen as bad and ugly.

Again, why the cross? Why the whipping? Why the thorns? Why all the bloodshed? Christ was dying to ask the same questions. "Why do you come out with swords and clubs and treat me like a criminal? I was with you every day in the temple, and you didn't arrest me. But this is your time, and *darkness is in control*" (Luke 22:52-53, CEV).

Why did you strike me? (John 18:23, NIV)

Why did you spit in my face?

Why did you nail my hands and feet to the beams?

Why did you make jokes about me as I hung suspended in the air?

Why the cross? Because *we* chose it for Him. Humanity screamed, "Crucify Him!" Just because He was willing to take what we dished out, didn't mean He wanted it that way. *Darkness was in control*, not God. Jesus tried reaching Judas' heart before he betrayed Him. God tried stopping Pilate's involvement by sending a dream to his wife (Matthew27:19). He tried to warn us where our hatred was taking us, but we didn't want to listen.

Jesus did not walk down a hardware store aisle and say, "I'll take three six-inch nails, a few wooden beams, and I wonder if they are out of the crown of thorns." He didn't choose the cross, we did. He was willing, however, to accept our choice for Him. Satan, sin, and sinners demanded Jesus' blood, and He willingly gave it. That He was *willing* to accept our *will* for Him, didn't mean He wanted it that way. Jesus could have given His life anywhere, but He chose to give it at the place of our choice. God gave His Son into the hands of a people whose hearts and minds were shrouded in the darkness of jealousy, fear, and anger, and it was that darkness that fastened Christ to a cross.

p.s. "The final prayer of Jesus was about you. His final pain was for you. His final passion was for you. Before He went to the cross, Jesus went to the garden. And when He spoke with His Father, you were in His prayers. ... And God couldn't turn His back on you. He couldn't because He saw you, and one look at you was all it took to convince Him. Right there in the middle of a world which isn't fair. He saw you cast into a river of life you didn't request. He saw you with a body which gets sick and a heart which grows weak. ... On the eve of the cross, Jesus made His decision. He would rather go to hell for you than go to heaven without you." —Max Lucado

Chapter 9

—— **Entangled with Grace** ——

"If anyone does not remain in me, he is like a branch that is thrown away and withers. ... " John 15:6, NIV

My mom was sitting in the loft directly behind the minister, adorned in a maroon choir robe. My brothers and I were seated about fifteen rows back, in the congregation, giggling as we drew funny pictures on the back of the church bulletins. This seemed like the only way to pass the time during a sermon that should have ended an hour earlier. The preacher seemed angry about something, as he shouted about how good God was and how we'd better obey Him. At that very moment, I felt a familiar burning sensation on the top of my lowered head. Mom would use her fiery, piercing eyes of discernment anytime she saw too much of our hair and not enough of our attentive eyes. My brothers and I would smell the burning flesh of our scalps, and look up in unison at the preacher and say, "Amen!" Mom would continue to stare at us with a look that said, "If you don't get your act together, so help me, I'm going to ..." For my mother, my A.D.D. communicated the highest disrespect and irreverence towards God. And if I thought my actions angered my mother, I knew they must have infuriated God. We all know what happens when God gets angry; cities explode, floods destroy, people run for their lives, and little irreverent boys get spanked.

These People Will Self-Destruct in 10...9...8...

The Bible hasn't always offered the best public relations service for God. He is often portrayed as an intimidator who is willing to fight with anyone bold enough to challenge His authority. Get Him angry and jealous enough, and His temper may even rain down fire from the sky.

The Bible includes many stories of destruction and violence. Some of our most uplifting stories from its pages involve someone, or many, losing their lives. The children of Israel being delivered from the Egyptians' captivity, the battle for the Promised Land, David's triumph over the giant, Goliath, Samson playing superhero on the Philistines, Noah and the flood, and especially, Jesus dying on the cross all illustrate horrific scenes of savagery. No wonder people make up their own versions of God. The one in scripture portrays a rather gruesome portrait of Him at times. Why does God seem to be in the middle of all these bloody pages?

For the most part, we simply don't understand God's interactions with people in scripture. For example, the Bible tells us before the flood every living person's thoughts were evil (Genesis 6:5). Imagine that— every person! Do you think it would have been more loving for God to step back and let the earthlings continue to terrorize one another? No. He had to stop evil. The cities of the earth were ruthless and cruel. Thievery and murder happened as often as breathing. Children were being sacrificed, women were being raped in the name of religion, and the poor were grossly neglected. If He hadn't stepped in, we would not be here today.

God found a good man named Noah. He instructed Him to build a large boat to travel in once the flood came. It took Noah 120 years to build that boat, and everyday he shared God's message of love for humanity and His displeasure with sin. God wanted a fresh start with a group of faithful followers to stunt sin's growth. It was the most merciful thing he could have done. If left alone, this cancerous evil would have continued to spread unabated.

Only eight people stepped into the ark of safety. Only eight people were willing to preserve God's principles for life, wellness, and happiness. Fortunately for us, the *Eight is Enough* crew was all God needed to curb evil and start anew. The flood was not about world destruction; it was about world preservation.

No Pleasure in Destruction

God does not enjoy any part of the death of his people, no matter how cruel they may be. He is not playing a video game, blowing up things and exclaiming, "Cool!" However, His love and compassion for innocent victims of cruelty compels Him to respond in their defense. God prefers for hearts to be changed for the betterment of mankind. Death is not so much God's choice for a disillusioned people as much as it is their choice. Sin is what brings ruin and destruction, and God does all He can to save us from its catastrophic consequences. God says in the book of Ezekiel:

> Change your hearts and stop all your sinning so sin will not bring your ruin. Get rid of all the sins you have done, and get for yourselves a new heart and a new way of thinking. Why do you want to die, people of Israel? For I take no pleasure in the death of anyone, declares the Sovereign Lord. Repent and live! (Ezekiel 18:31-32, CEV, NIV)

God never wants any of us to experience death. No one story can illustrate this truth better than the story of Jonah. The prophet is commanded by God to preach to the wicked city of Ninevah, telling them that they will be destroyed in 40 days. Jonah agrees at first, but then mysteriously changes his mind, running off to Tarshish (modern day Spain). While in route to Spain there is a huge storm, and Jonah believes that God has sent this storm to kill him for being disobedient. So, at Jonah's urging, the reluctant sailors throw him overboard to appease God's wrath. What a crazy guy! Who gave him the idea that in order to pacify God's anger you must kill yourself? How barbaric!

Anyhow, Jonah is now sinking to his death, praying for his life. God, who never wanted to kill Jonah in the first place, proves this by using the powers of Aquaman. He summons a large fish to swallow Jonah in order to prevent him from drowning. After the fish spits Jonah safely onto the shore, a gratitude-filled Jonah rushes off to Nineveh to do the Lord's will.

After the people of Nineveh hear Jonah's sermon, they do something the people in Noah's day didn't do—they ask God for forgiveness. They change their ways. They repent. When God saw that their lives were changed, the Bible says He changed His mind also, and did not bring about the destruction he said He would (Jonah 3:10). I know you thought God never changed His mind (Mal. 3:6), but read why He does:

> And if I say to the wicked man, 'You will surely die,' but he then turns away from his sin and does what is just and right— if he gives back what he took in pledge for a loan, returns what he has stolen, follows the decrees that give life, and does no evil, he will surely live; he will not die. None of the sins he has

committed will be remembered against him. He has done what is just and right; he will surely live. (Ezekiel 33:14-16, NIV)

In another place God also says:

If I threaten to uproot and shatter an evil nation and that nation turns from its evil, I will change my mind. If I promise to make a nation strong, but its people start disobeying me and doing evil, then I will change my mind and not help them at all. (Jeremiah 18:7-9, CEV)

When God says He does not change, He is speaking of His character. But His decisions are always subject to change because people are always subject to change. His motives behind His decisions, however, never change. They are always motivated by love.

There is a twist in this story, though. Jonah becomes furious when God forgives the people of Nineveh, and finally tells us the real reason why he fled to Spain.

Didn't I say before I left home that you would do this, Lord? That is why I ran away to Tarshish! I knew that you are a merciful and compassionate God, slow to get angry and filled with unfailing love. You are eager to turn back from destroying people. Just kill me now, Lord! I'd rather be dead than alive if what I predicted will not happen. (Jonah 4:2-3, NLT)

What a wonderful God! What unfailing love! For Jonah to say something like that implies this is not the first time God has done something like this. It is His mode of operation. He has a reputation for grace. Jonah, who days earlier was a recipient of God's mercy and compassion, is tired of God being nice to *really* bad people. But that is just who God is. He even loves His enemies, and there is nothing we can do about it.

God's response to Jonah's complaint is, "Shouldn't I show concern for the great city Nineveh, which has more than one hundred twenty thousand people who do not know right from wrong, and many animals, too?" (Jonah 4:11, NCV). God was looking out for all the innocent people, as well as all the precious animals in the city. How thoughtful it is when someone's pet hamster gets consideration and concern from the Creator. He is a defender for the defenseless. Every decision God makes is weighed with the utmost measure of sensitivity and kindness. God uprooted wicked cities in love and mercy, and He also spared them for the same reasons.

Grace on the Menu

Israel, through the help of the prophet Elisha, had trapped an enemy army and was ready to rid themselves of their unfriendly antagonist. When the king of Israel asked the prophet if they had permission to kill them, God's response through the prophet was classic. "'Of course not! ... Do we kill prisoners of war? Give them food and drink and send them home again to their master.' So the king made a great feast for them and then sent them home to their master." (2 Kings 6:22-23, NLT)

Israel's soldiers dropped their weapons, placed menus on the table, picked up a pen and pad and asked, "Would you like to hear our specials for today?" Outstanding! I thought with this enemy army firmly in His grasp, God would have finished them off. No, instead of slaughtering them, God opens up the five-star restaurant Graceau (it's French). God is relentless in seeking every possible avenue to be merciful and compassionate.

The Devil Made Me Do It

As much as we misunderstand God and His dealings with erring people, we equally forget about Satan's involvement within these same circumstances. Part of the reason for this is the way in which the biblical authors viewed God and the universe. They believed that because God authorizes everything that takes place under the sun, He must be held ultimately responsible for everything that happens. For instance, Jonah accuses God of throwing him into the ocean even though it was the sailors who actually did it after Jonah had repeatedly suggested for them to do so (Jonah 2:3). There are numerous occasions in the Bible where God is credited with an action He never committed—only permitted.

The most recognizable case of mistaken identity is recorded in two different places in the Bible—2 Samuel 24 and 1 Chronicles 21. The book of Samuel presents the idea that God was angry with Israel and was looking for an excuse to punish them. So he provoked David to take a census. David did so, with the intent of sizing up his army, therefore showing his trust in the strength of Israel rather than faith in the power of God. Israel was then punished, essentially, for what God had pushed David to do. Now does that make sense? God tempts us to fail so He can punish us for the failure? The author of the Chronicles' version writes more accurately that *Satan* rose up against Israel and provoked David to take the census. Now that makes sense. Satan is the tempter, not God (James 1:13). One author credits God because He allowed it, and the other didn't believe that God should be held responsible just because He permitted it. Satan was the culprit, not God.

We don't give God's arch enemy enough liability concerning all the chaos in the world. Just because God is more powerful doesn't mean Satan has no power of his own. Remember when God let Satan afflict Job? He removed His hedge around Job and Satan seemed to have awesome powers to destroy his property, family, and health. Fire came out of the sky; winds were blowing stuff on top of people. It seems even Satan has command over nature and its elements when God removes His protection.

God removing His protection is the key factor here. Remember the story of the serpents attacking the rebellious Israelites in the desert? The snakes were already present in the desert. However, only when God removed His presence, and the Israelites no longer had His refuge, were they bitten by them. When God threatens to punish a rebellious people with famine, disease, or war, He doesn't actually do it Himself. All God does is remove His presence, and the inevitable happens—enemy armies invade, the people become susceptible to all kinds of diseases, and famine becomes a natural reality as it was with all the other nations.

I'm sure Satan salivates at the predicament of a God-less people, because the presence of the Lord is no longer there to protect them from his attacks. When the people pushed God away through their continual disobedience, He eventually gave the people what they wanted—freedom from Him. After Israel had broken their covenant with God for the umpteenth time and desired freedom from His laws, God declared, "I now proclaim 'freedom' for you—'freedom' to fall by the sword, plague, and famine" (Jeremiah 34:17). Freedom from God always leaves us open and vulnerable to Satan's attacks. Pushing God away is never a good idea. It is very likely that most of the perceived divine acts of destruction in the Bible occur only after God removes Himself from the situation. And when that happens, the lying spirit, angel of death, Satan, moves in for the attack.

You may not believe that bad things always happen when God removes Himself. You have observed many prosperous people in history and in the present who have disregarded every principle in the Bible, yet seem to be quite successful. Well, prosperity can be quite the weapon in the Devil's arsenal. Relationships, fame, wealth, and a high position at work can all be used by Satan to take us down. That is why I feel the popular saying "be careful what you wish for" deserves consideration as an honorary scriptural text. Sin never offers freedom or real prosperity—only enslavement (John 8:34, Romans 6:20-23).

It is the removal of God's presence that makes the weight of sin so unbearable and its consequences so excruciating. Anytime God steps back, Satan swoops in to have his way. Satan wants everyone destroyed. He is not trying to hold on to this world like some prized possession; he wants it obliterated. The Bible tells us that Satan roams around like a roaring lion wanting to devour us (1 Peter 5:8). He hates you and everything you love because his enemy loves you. If God were to remove His presence entirely, Satan would ravage the earth in minutes. God, however, is holding back the winds of devastation (Revelation 7:1). He isn't trying to destroy the earth under Satan's rule; rather, God has been preserving us within it. He is the buffer for evil so we do not feel the full brunt of it like He did at Calvary. But when He steps back, all hell breaks loose.

The Second Boat

Considering the outcome of the Jonah story, if the people had repented during Noah's time, God would have changed His mind and not sent the flood. They didn't repent, so God continued with *Operation Mercy* through other means. The curious thing is God waited seven days from the closing of the Ark's door before sending the first drop of rain. And no, it wasn't to test the faith of Noah and his family. I think 120 years of building that boat was enough evidence of the family's faith. Seven more days was not going to shake it. I'd like to think God waited a little longer for the people who remained outside the boat. I imagine there was another opportunity for mercy; that some hearts, through sincere repentance, were turned to God even after He closed the door. They missed the *first* boat, but here was a chance not to miss the *second* one. They experienced the first death (just a sleep) for sure, but maybe they will not have to experience the second death on judgment day (eternal sleep). There were those who didn't accept Christ during His first coming. Yet, after the disciples' ministry many repented of rejecting Christ, and will accept Him at His second coming. God's grace has a way of giving people multiple opportunities for change.

I'm sure in all these violent stories in the Bible there were innocent people who perished. Whether by God's command, Satan's attacks, or through the cruelty of humanity, I know there were innocent children who died. Like we have discussed before, this is the part of life that never feels fair. Even so, I am convinced God will save every innocent life that perished. God will make it up to every little girl, boy, woman or man who died in a war, flood, earthquake, accident, or from an untimely illness. God healed Job and blessed him and his wife with more children, wealth, and prosperity than before. And let's not forget, Jesus also called Lazarus back to life. One day soon every stone will be rolled away, and Christ will call every innocent person back to life. He will remove the entangling grave clothes of this sinful world forever. He promises to make it up to everyone.

I have a hunch there will be no complaints after Jesus returns to make all things new, and gives the *redeemed* the keys to their mansions He has prepared for them (John 14:1-3, KJV). I have a feeling when they look at His nail-scarred hands, they'll know He was also once an innocent victim of violence; and through His own shed blood, Jesus purchased a life of true freedom and real happiness.

p.s. Christ is a death survivor. And through His grace, so will we all be.

Chapter 10

—— *Godzilla* ——

"Such branches are picked up, thrown into the fire and burned." John 15:6, NIV

Superman was my favorite superhero growing up. He was a big nice guy with blue tights and a long red cape (loved the cape). He often reminded me of how I imagined Jesus, saving the world using his super powers, all the while sporting a big smile on his face. Among all Superman's powers, his heat-vision was one of my favorites. He could literally shoot fire out of his eyes. The Man of Steel would use his heat-vision to protect and save people. Although as time rolled on, our society seemed to reject the smiling, "campy" superhero characters of our parents' generation for edgier, darker representations of those personas. Batman and Wolverine were far cooler than Superman and Captain America because they had a bad boy streak in them. Who wants to be a boy scout when you could be the cool guy with the tattoos and shades riding a Harley-Davidson (or Batmobile)? Even the bad guys in the movies began to be presented in such a way that you would find yourself rooting for them instead of the good guys. So to adapt to our changing culture, the classic Boy Scout hero, Superman, was given a more fear-striking look. Many artists began to portray him with glowing red eyes, as if he were ready, eager if you will, to blast you with the fire emitting from them. Being an art enthusiast myself, I would look at these new representations and exclaim, "Awesome!" I liked the darker look. I was the kid who much preferred Darth Vader to Luke Skywalker.

Although I felt my Superman looked "cooler" with the glowing red eyes, I didn't like that look for God. The Bible describes our loving friend, Jesus, in the book of Revelation, as having eyes "like blazing fire" (Rev. 1:14, NIV). That text didn't make Him look cooler to me, but rather scarier. I felt like those fiery eyes were fixated right on me. I was Lex Luthor, and God was waiting for me to make one wrong move, then "Blast!"

I felt forced into submission. I had to be His friend. I had to accept His commandments. I had to accept His will for my life. I had to accept His death on the cross. It seemed unfair to me. Just because God had super powers didn't give Him the right to blast everyone who disagreed with Him, did it?

A Bit Overdone

God's acts of grace are quite inspiring. As you find yourself warming up to Him though, you can't help but notice the warmth getting uncomfortably warmer. There is a voice in the back of your mind that keeps whispering reminders of a hot place that God has prepared for those who disobey Him. It is then when we stop moving closer to God, and instead look suspiciously at His extended hand—the one supposedly offered in friendship. It is difficult to accept His friendship when we believe He has a smoking flamethrower behind His back saying, "Accept me, or I'll pull the trigger."

Now don't get me wrong—I don't have a problem with the picture of God disciplining people. God "disciplines those He loves" (Proverbs 3:12, NIV). And as we have already learned, it would be cruel of God to not give evil any boundaries. However, there is a difference between discipline and abuse. Discipline is always given for the purpose of correcting detrimental behavior. Giving a child a time-out can be considered a reasonable corrective, disciplinary action, but children getting beat with the heel of a hard shoe may be deemed a bit abusive.

I remember my parents telling me to go pick out a branch from the tree, prune it (in Latin this was called a "switch"), and bring it back into the house so I could be spanked with it (so glad those days are over). That was a widely accepted practice of discipline when I was a child. Today, however, there are many who would disagree. I don't have a problem with discipline, but I do with abuse.

So far we have looked at the reasons why God, in love, would place boundaries for wickedness. But what in the *Hades* do we do with the concept of hell? Our traditional view of hell's blazing inferno, where sinners go to burn forever, is abuse times infinity. No other Christian doctrine has done more to scare people away from God or made them serve Him out of fear than this understanding of hell. It is a disturbing teaching because it seems to contradict our belief in a loving God. Even a hateful God wouldn't be that cruel. We can understand the principles behind discipline and justice, but how can anyone explain a place of never-ending torment?

If discipline is corrective, who is God correcting in the end? It's not like the wicked are going to say while burning forever, "We are never going to mess up like this again!" They will not have any more opportunities for change. Therefore, hell could not be seen as a disciplinary act since there is no possibility for correction. It's not as if the righteous people need to see this mass capital punishment to keep them in line for eternity. They have already made up their mind to trust God, so they do not need any external motivation at this point. And it's not as if God's followers are demanding this type of justice, because they would not wish this type of torture on their worst enemy.

Fear Tactics

The whole idea of God being abusive makes me think that our loving Creator flips a switch and blows His top in the end. If God is forcing me into a relationship with Him by scaring me into submission, then I don't want to have anything to do with Him. You cannot tell me you love me and I better be your friend or else you're going to kill me. And, not just kill me, but also work a miracle within my body so that I can burn forever in some big microwave. All because I didn't learn to love and trust you? That is why so many of our relationships with God are unhealthy and dysfunctional. They're prefaced on fear.

God does not use fear tactics to influence our decision to accept Him. If that were His idea, He would have shown up as the seventy-foot giant Godzilla and blown fire out of His nostrils. The whole world would follow Him if He did that. They would be impressed with His awesome power and might. They would be intimidated by His size and influence. But they would not love Him. They would serve Him, but they sure would not want to be friends with Him. Instead, God showed up as a baby.

The closest I've come to wielding a weapon of fear was when I had to creatively encourage my youngest brother, Rafik, to follow my instructions. The way I used to get my baby bro' to obey me during his *terrible two's* stage was to pull out this old, rusty, red vacuum from the closet, turn the beast on, and chase him around the house (I know—shame on me). There was no speech about how this was going to hurt me more than him. Just a reach for the closet door would usually do the trick. *"Do you want me to unleash the red monster, boy? Don't make me wake him up!"* Rafik was so scared of that vacuum that he would do whatever I asked of him.

Is that the kind of obedience God wants from us? He could have destroyed Lucifer (Satan) from the beginning, but the rest of the universe would have thought, "You better follow God or He'll vacuum you up!" He didn't want anyone to be in a relationship with Him because they were afraid of what He would do to them if they said no. If God didn't use that method in the beginning, He surely won't use it in the end. "There is *no fear in love*. But perfect love drives out fear, because fear has to do with punishment" (1 John 4:18, NIV).

Now there is a passage that *seemingly* contradicts John's view on God concerning fear. Jesus is recorded as urging His followers: "Do not be afraid of those who kill the body but cannot kill the soul. Rather, be afraid of *the one* who can destroy both soul and body in hell" (Matthew 10:28, NIV). Many believe "the one" Jesus is referring to is His Father. I used the word *seemingly* because in the very next verse Jesus reminds His disciples that just as the Father has a tender watchful eye on every sparrow, He has also numbered even the very hairs on their head. "So *don't be afraid*; you are worth more than many sparrows" (Matthew 10:31, NIV). I think it is highly unlikely Jesus would tell His disciples to fear God, and in the next breath, say, "Oops, I mean don't fear Him." Maybe the one we are to fear is not God, but someone or something else.

Earning our respect and friendship means too much to God. If love is not the compelling force that draws us to Him, then He won't seek to win our affection in any other way. God declares, "I want *faithful love* more than I want animal sacrifices. I want people *to know me* more than I want burnt offerings" (Hosea 6:6, NCV).

Burn, Baby, Burn

So what do we do with these intense images of everlasting fire and torment? They are in the Bible. Well, let's take a closer look. God had threatened to destroy the walls of Jerusalem with an unquenchable fire (Jeremiah 17:27), and the Babylonians eventually did burn them down, but are the walls still burning today? An everlasting fire destroyed Sodom, but it's not burning anymore (Jude 7). When the Bible describes fire as unquenchable, or everlasting, it simply means it will burn until it has accomplished its purpose. Firefighters will not be able to douse the flames. The fire burns until there is no more wood in the fireplace. And when it is used to describe the finality of sin, the *result* of the destruction is everlasting; the *process,* however, is not.

Now, I have to admit, I still don't like the idea of God tossing people into a fireplace. Can you imagine God tying someone to a stake, dousing him or her with gasoline, then lighting the match? Me neither. That is just sadistic. I know some say, "God has to repay the wicked back for what they did." With that in mind, should He erect some crosses and nail His former tormentors there? Doesn't that make God look petty? He would look like a little boy throwing rocks at another boy who threw rocks at Him. The picture of God getting even makes Him look so childish and too much like us. I thought God was supposed to be bigger than us? Thankfully, He is. When it comes to mercy and judgment, God is nothing like us.

> Return to the LORD our God. He will be merciful and forgive your sins. The LORD says: "My thoughts and my ways are not like yours. Just as the heavens are higher than the earth, my thoughts and my ways are higher than yours." (Isaiah 55:7-9, NIV)

> I will not carry out my fierce anger, nor will I turn and devastate. … For I am God, *and not man*—the Holy One among you. I will not come in wrath. (Hosea 11:9, NIV)

The God who tells us to love our enemies would not, Himself, do any less. God's way of handling the wicked should be as jaw-droppingly merciful as He was with the Aramean army and the city of Ninevah. Could you ever imagine building an oven to throw your children, spouse, or best friend into if they mistreated you? Can you see yourself turning the heat up and hearing them scream in pain? It's revolting to even give it a thought. A person once told me, "I would never do that, but I'm not God." *Yeah,* I thought, *you're worse.* Sinners cannot be more compassionate than God. Mercy is His middle name. He would never do anything that would even be beneath us. Remember, His ways are *higher* than ours, not below.

Garbage Dump

So where does this whole idea of hell come from? Jesus refers to hell in the Greek as *Gehenna,* which was the name of the ever-burning garbage dump near Jerusalem. That got my wheels turning. Who better to talk about this subject than Jesus? Gehenna, or hell, was the local city dump where people would throw away all their trash and the dead bodies of those whose families couldn't afford a proper burial place. Executed criminals were often thrown in there. Jesus' body would have also been taken there after His death had it not been for one of His rich friends that begged Pilate for a proper burial site (Mark 15:43).

Do you get it? Hell is a place where dead people burned. Jesus' illustration of the vine in John 15:6 have the branches being thrown away, withering (which is death), and then they are cast into the fire. Isaiah 66 and Revelation 20, which are the most popular chapters about the end of evil, both describe *dead* bodies being consumed by a fire, or being tossed into a lake of fire.

> And they will go out and look upon the dead bodies of those who rebelled against me; their worm will not die, nor will their fire be quenched, and they will be loathsome to all mankind. (Isaiah 66:24, NIV)

> Then death and Hades [world of the dead] were thrown into the lake of fire. The lake of fire is the second death. (Revelation 20:14, NIV)

God does not torture living people with fire; He cleanses that which is already dead. These verses are also steeped in symbolism and metaphors. Are these worms that don't die fire retardant? Why would *death* be thrown into the lake of fire if it is not an actual person? Isn't it interesting that Revelation 20:14 tells us that the lake of fire *is* the second death? God is confined to our language to describe with symbols, metaphors, and parables something that is almost indescribable. But all the biblical imagery—worms that don't die, unquenchable fire, chains of darkness (2 Peter 2:4), outer darkness, and weeping and gnashing of teeth (Matt 8:12) all communicate the same idea: We don't want to have anything to do with sin or its inevitable consequences.

Separation Anxiety

Well, then how do the wicked die? I can answer that with a question: How did Jesus die? It wasn't the cross that killed Christ. He died when the Father turned away (Psalm 22:1, Matthew 27:46). This was the cup Jesus did not want to drink in the Garden of Gethsemane (Matthew 26:39, 42); the cup of God's wrath the book of Revelation says will be poured out on the wicked (Revelation 14:10). When the Father withdrew, the Son's heart was crushed. That is the price of sin—the final result of sin. When the people make their final decision to turn away from God, they will be cut-off from the Vine. They will wither away and die. "They will be punished with eternal destruction, [which is] *forever separated* from the Lord and from his glorious power" (2 Thessalonians 1:9, NLT).

Jesus experienced the death of a lost sinner. He felt as if his separation from the Father was permanent. The price of sin is not to be crucified or burned forever. The price of sin is to be eternally separated from God. Once you are disconnected from the source of life, everlasting death is inevitable. This is the "strange act" of God (Isaiah 28:21, KJV). Strange in that it will be the first and last time God is forever separated from His creation.

Why would God allow His children to be cut-off forever? It is actually what they prefer. John writes, "And now, little children, abide in Him, that when He appears, we may have *confidence* and not be ashamed before Him at His coming" (1 John 2:28, KJV). The Bible tells us the ashamed will cry for the rocks to crush them (Revelation 6:16). This is the "weeping and gnashing of teeth" that Jesus describes the lost will experience in the end. Their mental and emotional suffering are so painful and torturous that they cry out for death. We should not fear God, but rather sin and its inevitable consequences. This is the natural end result for those who "break-up" with God. It is this agonizing moment that God is so desperately trying to save everyone from, including Himself. It breaks His heart as much as it crushes theirs, as the Creator separates from His creation.

When Jesus returns to this earth, He will raise up His friends who are sleeping in their graves. Those of us who are still alive will put on our red capes and be "caught up" to meet Him in the air (1 Thessalonians 4:13-17). What a scene, as millions of people meet Jesus in the air. We know Him. He's our Friend. We look forward to spending eternity with Him. However, those who do not know God will be afraid of Him. They run in the opposite direction. Sadly, there will be those who want nothing to do with God's rescue mission. They didn't care to know Him in this life, and nothing will change their hearts now.

They are unconverted. God can smile all He wants, but He is still a big stranger to them. He is Godzilla, breathing fire.

Should God take the people running away from Him to heaven anyway? Remember, they didn't like or trust Him here on Earth, so they won't like or trust Him there. Life would not be on their terms, so it wouldn't be a pleasant place to live. In her book *Steps to Christ*, Ellen White conjured that heaven would be a place of torture for the unchanged sinner.

In his sinless state, man held joyful communion with [God] 'in whom are hid all the treasures of wisdom and knowledge.' Colossians 2:3. But after his sin, he could no longer find joy in holiness, and he sought to hide from the presence of God. Such is still the condition of the unrenewed heart. It is not in harmony with God, and finds no joy in communion with Him. The sinner could not be happy in God's presence; he would shrink from the companionship of holy beings. Could he be permitted to enter heaven, it would have no joy for him. The spirit of unselfish love that reigns there –every heart responding to the heart of Infinite Love –would touch no answering chord in his soul. His thoughts, his interests, his motives, would be alien to those that actuate the sinless dwellers there. He would be a discordant note in the melody of heaven. Heaven would be to him a place of torture; he would long to be hidden from Him who is its light, and the center of its joy. It is no arbitrary decree on the part of God that excludes the wicked from heaven; they are shut out by their own unfitness for its companionship. The glory of God would be to them a consuming fire. They would welcome destruction, that they might be hidden from the face of Him who died to redeem them.

If God really wanted to punish the guilty, He would send them to heaven. However, that would be too cruel for even God to do. For the wicked, heaven would not be a place of good times. Should God let them live on their own planet by themselves? Heavens, no! That would be hell! Can you imagine living through the last stages of cancer for eternity? Your liver explodes from alcoholism, but you cannot die from it because you have eternal life on your new planet. Imagine battling with depression where no amount of exercise, medication, or counseling can help. And just in case you felt you could take your life to end all the suffering, remember God has granted you the gift of living forever. And you thought this world was unfair? They do not want to live with God, nor live without Him. "There was no place for them" (Revelation 20:11, NIV). They only want one thing. Only death can bring them peace. So with tears in His eyes, God *finally* turns away.

It is not that these lost people weren't good enough to be saved. It's just that they didn't know Him as well as you and I do, nor did they want to. They never trusted the Creator's blueprints for happiness. It's not that they weren't forgiven, because Christ also died for their sins. It's just that they were unwilling to trust in God's forgiveness. As a result, their hearts became as hard as the stone in front of Lazarus' tomb. There was nothing more God could do for them. So, His last act of mercy is to give them relief from their misery.

The lost actually worship God for His goodness before He departs from them forever. It's almost as if they are grateful for Him putting them out of their misery. Even when God is presumably at his worst, the wicked feel He is at His best and deserving of worship. "Every knee bows and every tongue confesses He is Lord" (Rom 14:11, NIV). This time, death is not just a momentary sleep—it is *everlasting*. They will never rise again. Satan and his angels will never rise again. They would not have it any other way.

Just when we thought God could not possibly show any more love or mercy towards sinners; just when we thought He could not give any more than He did at Calvary, He comes at the end of time for an encore. An encore of grace, where the wicked receive peace from their suffering through death, and the friends of God receive peace from their suffering through everlasting life with Christ. What a wonderful God!

p.s. I know there is a small, vindictive part in all of us that is crying, "Unfair!" We're thinking that the wicked are getting off too easy. However, when we consider Calvary, didn't we all get off too easy?

— Postscript —

"I no longer call you servants, because a servant does not know his master's business. Instead, I have called you friends, for everything that I learned from my Father I have made known to you." John 15:15, NIV

A pastor was asked by one of his church members to spend time with her deathly-ill father. The pastor obliged and visited her father, Frank, in the hospital. He walked into a warm, sun-lit hospital room with only one bed. The room soon became chilly when the old man told the pastor that he was wasting his time. "I don't believe in God," he bitterly muttered. The pastor said, "That's fine. I just want to sit next to you and keep you company." The two cordially talked about sports and politics, and even shared a few laughs about their similar upbringings. Eventually Frank began to entrust the pastor with his doubts concerning God and the reasons he found it so hard to believe in Him. The pastor did his best to make things clearer for Frank. He spoke of God's love for him and His desire to rid the world of sin forever. He spoke of God's perfect will and His promise to return everything to perfect harmony. He spoke about the price of redemption and how much worth and value God's places on Frank's life.

As the pastor was preparing himself to leave, Frank asked him, "How can I talk to God?" The pastor smiled, got up from his chair and scooted it closer to the bed. "Imagine God sitting right here in this chair, Frank, and talk to Him as you would to a friend."

A few weeks later the pastor received a phone call from Frank's daughter. The emotional and trembling voice on the other end shared that her father had passed away. After the pastor had given his condolences, the daughter felt compelled to share the peculiar position in which they found her dead father. "We walked into the room," she said, "and found his body draped around the chair by the bed. Pastor, he died with his arms around the chair."

Friend, there is a whole new world of experiences full of joy and happiness awaiting you. Maybe you attempted to know God before, but after staring at the picture a little longer, you finally see Him for who He really is. Isn't He worth another try? Maybe you have never experienced a friendship with Him. Isn't it time you begin one?

Guess Who's Coming to Dinner?

In a parable about heaven, Jesus describes to His friends what it will be like for those who know Him, and are prepared for His return. "Be ready and keep your lamps burning just like those servants who wait up for their master to return from a wedding feast. As soon as he comes and knocks, they open the door for him. Servants are fortunate if their master finds them awake and ready when he comes! *I promise you* that he will get ready and have his servants sit down so he can serve them" (Luke 12:35-37, CEV).

What a beautiful picture of God. Just when I thought we would be the ones clamoring over Him when we are brought into His kingdom, He flips the script and He clamors over us. We should wait on Him, but He prefers to wait on us.

We are at a long banquet table, and our server is none other than the Son of God. He places the menu in our hands and recommends that we choose the special for the day. Want to know what it is? It is fruit from the Tree of Life. You're probably thinking that item on the menu is too expensive. Don't worry; your Server has already picked up the tab. It was charged to His account. He has the receipt of payment in His hands. He rubs our shoulders as He thanks us, one by one, for trusting Him. He thanks us for taking the time for a closer look.

Finally, Jesus arrives at your seat. He places His hands on your shoulders and gives them a little rub of gratitude. There is so much strength, yet tenderness in His touch. Your mind wanders as you contemplate how those same hands have comforted, healed, and guided so many in life. Placing your hand on His, you turn around to thank Him. You pause as you feel the nail print in His hand. Compelled to look at the scar, your eyes well up with tears. Sensing your feelings of unworthiness, Jesus presses closer to you and whispers in that still small voice, *"You were worth every drop."*

— References —

- Bell, R. (2007). *Sex God*. Grand Rapids: Zondervan. p. 124
- De Mello, A. (1992). *The Way to Love*. New York: Doubleday. p. 2
- Lewis, C.S. (1980). *Mere Christianity*. New York: HarperCollins. p. 50
- Lucado, M. (2000). *Grace for the Moment*. Nashville: Thomas Nelson. p. 112
- *Merriam-Webster's Dictionary*. Springfield: Merriam-Webster.
- White, E. (1940). *The Desire of Ages*. Nampa: Pacific Press. p. 759
- White, E. (2000). *Steps to Christ*. Nampa: Pacific Press. p. 17
- Yaconelli, M. (2007). *Messy Spirituality*. Grand Rapids: Zondervan. p. 19
- Yancey, P. (2006). *Prayer: What Difference Does It Make?* Grand Rapids: Zondervan. p. 36

— Thank you —

Writing does not come easy for me, so I must acknowledge those who assisted me in making this vision become a reality.

Thank you, Dex (D. Roderick!!!), for pushing me to paint this picture of God on a readable canvas. I can never repay you for your dedication to this project and your enthusiasm for this message (although I'm sure you'll think of something). You must have read all of my drafts at least twenty times, but always made it feel as if you were reading it for the first time. Your developmental editing and spiritual guidance was invaluable. You're my friend, brother, and pastor.

Thank you, Iris, for your enthusiasm and commitment to the book. Thank you for putting up with all of my last minute changes as you helped in the editing process. Your support in the finishing stages is what kept me going.

Thank you, Sheila, for never being too busy to talk about the subject that is most important to me—Jesus. This book is a result of hours of our conversations. "Put the bulletin away and come down for the appeal." (ily3x;-)

Thank you, Greta (auntie), for contributing your time, energy, and expertise in the last stages of editing. Thank you for cooking the vegetarian Scallops that helped fuel me through the long nights of writing. With aunties like you, what else could I possibly need?

Thank you, Judi, for coming through at the stroke of midnight to add all of the finishing touches. Your suggestions were spot on. It was all divine providence.

I thank you, church family ("The Grand" Avenue Seventh-Day Adventist Church), for all your support. You make being your pastor fun. Thank you, Ryan, for your thoughtful, sometimes brutal, critique of the first draft. You helped set the course. Thank you, *Las Hermanas*, for the feedback and the fun breaks from writing (pupusas anyone?). Thank you Johnson sisters, Mel-o-die, Mindy, Laura, Karina, Miriam, Jean, Nathaela, and Dr. Roland Hsu for all your critiques of the first draft. Thank you, Preston, for helping me with the cover of the book. And for everyone else that contributed in some way, even if to give me a break, sincere thanks from the bottom of my heart.

Extended Thanks
Thank you family ...

Mom, you are incredible and I love you so much. You are the closest example of God in my life (minus the pillowcases).

Dad, you are the most thoughtful man I know. I still want to grow up and be like you one day.

Bobby, you truly are the best. What would growing up be like without you? *Boring.* Proud of you, man.

Greg, you are a gift. You make life truly worth living. All my favorite memories have you in it.

Rafik, you are more like me than you think (except for the red vacuum stuff). I'm glad I get to be a part of your life.

Jean, where would I be if I never brought you that glass of OJ at age two? Thank you for your love and support.

La La and Michelle, thank you for all you have done in my life. You mean so much to me.

Thank you, Max and William, for making life full of laughs and fun. Basketball and videogames can still be quite the combination.

Thank you to all of my cousins, aunts, and uncles. You all know very well how you have blessed me immeasurably.

Grandparents, where would I be without your love and commitment? I know a bit of what heaven will be like having spent time in your home. Thank you can never express my deep gratitude and love for you.

Thank you, Pacific Union College. I experienced a transformation on your campus that is still evident today. I wish I could attend another four years there. Keep reaching the world for Christ, one student at a time.

To order sermons, books, or to schedule speaking appointments by Jonathan Henderson please visit www.grandadvent.org or e-mail office@grandadvent.org